OLD HOUSES
ON NANTUCKET

The front entry — 33 Milk Street

OLD HOUSES
ON
NANTUCKET

by Kenneth Duprey

The parlor — 139 Main Street

Architectural Book Publishing Co., Inc.

NEW YORK

Distributed to the book trade by
National Book Network, Inc.

LIBRARY OF CONGRESS CATALOG CARD NUMBER: 59-10847
ISBN: 0-942655-14-1

Printed in China

Contents

TO ALICE VAN LEER CARRICK,
WHOSE BOOK, *THE NEXT-TO-NOTHING HOUSE,*
BEGAN MY LIFE LONG INTEREST IN OLD HOUSES

Preface

WHEN, some twelve years ago, I first acquired an old house in Nantucket Town and set about to repair the damage from several decades of natural deterioration and human redecoration, I found there existed no adequate descriptions of the architecture or interior furnishing of this type of house which is peculiar to the island and is as distinctive in its way as the better-known Cape Cod cottage. Here was a chapter of American architectural history which was as yet unwritten. It is still not written, for here are only some of the materials which will go into its composition. But in the course of reclaiming one old house, I found it necessary to examine, compare and photograph other old houses on the island, and from these study materials, gathered for a practical purpose, has come the present volume which I hope will still have a practical purpose for other householders, not only on Nantucket but any place where honest architecture is appreciated.

While compiling such a volume as this, I have been indebted to many persons, not the least of which are the householders who have generously allowed me to photograph their homes for a publication. Their names will be found listed in the volume. If I have included pictures of my own house at 26 Milk Street, it is not because I rate it so high among the many from which I have had to choose, but because I have in the course of years become thoroughly familiar with its construction and appreciative of many details which only daily living calls to one's attention.

My indebtedness to the many who have written about Nantucket is only partially discharged in the bibliography at the end of the volume, which includes some of the books I have found especially useful. I am grateful to Miss

Grace Brown Gardner, who has allowed me to make frequent use of her invaluable scrapbooks on island history, and to the Society for the Preservation of New England Antiquities, which has generously put its archives at my disposal and permitted the reproduction of the old photograph of the house at 138 Center Street. For the old photographs of West Brick I am indebted to the kindness of Mrs. Lincoln J. Ceely, and to *Popular Photography* for permission to reproduce the photograph of the back stair of the house at 10 Gardner Street. In conclusion, I wish to thank Dr. John L. Bishop for editing and Miss Jean Purdon for preparing the manuscript for press and to express my appreciation to Mr. Marshall H. Sheldon for his interest and diplomacy which have encouraged and lightened the task of taking these photographs over many years.

K. D.

Introduction

FROM Nantucket, a tiny island off the New England coast, sailed rugged ships manned partly by Quaker crews to hunt the whale in oceans around the globe. Here was once one of the greatest whaling ports in the world and a stronghold of the Quaker sect. Gone now is the bustle of a major commercial port, and gone is the Quaker domination, but the buildings remain to tell the story of a vigorous past and to offer us an unusually fine study of a domestic, regional architecture.

Concentrated in an area approximately fifteen miles long and five miles wide at its broadest point, is an architectural development extending in time from the last quarter of the seventeenth century to the middle of the nineteenth century, from the primitive, early colonial Jethro Coffin House on Sunset Hill overlooking the present town, to the stately Greek Revival mansions on Main Street. These were Nantucket's energetic years that produced the indigenous architecture, now its principal attraction.

In general, the development of the island's architecture paralleled, with modifications, that of the mainland and falls into five periods, convenient for the historian but actually overlapping and never sharply defined. The story of this domestic architecture is told in the following pages by photographs of exteriors and interiors, captioned and accompanied by a minimum of intrusive text. Measured drawings have been included, even though the book is intended for the layman rather than the architect or architectural historian. Such drawings have been limited to that section of the book which considers a purely local product, the typical Nantucket house, that developed as a result of Quaker influence during the second half of the eighteenth century. The island architecture before and after this period differs from that on the mainland only in minor details, and drawings of these differences would interest only the specialist with an inclination for splitting hairs. As far as possible I have used the old names for the various rooms of a house, and the reader will find at the end of the volume a glossary of architectural terms and expressions peculiar to the island which occur in the text.

Nantucket is fortunate in not being a reconstruction or a restoration. Its dwellings, homes of islanders and others who have adopted the island as a home, still shelter their owners, as they have for centuries, from the elements of which Nantucket, because of its exposed location far out to sea, has more than its share. Many of the houses pictured in this book are not accessible to the public, and it is hoped that the privacy of their owners, who have so kindly allowed these interiors to be made public, will continue to be respected. Those houses that are open to the public offer a fine cross section of the island's architectural heritage and are well worth visiting. All of them have been included here.

The houses in this volume have been presented, as far as possible, in chronological order. It is hoped that they will provide both the knowing and the architecturally uninitiated with an entertaining and instructive tour of the island's old dwellings, helping him to understand more fully and appreciate a fascinating segment of American regional architecture and to increase his enjoyment of that unique dot in the Atlantic at latitude 41° 16′ 36″, west longitude 70° 6′ 06″ called Nantucket Island.

A List of Houses and Householders

[1]Owners at the time the photographs, here reprinted by the courtesy of Mrs. Lincoln J. Ceeley, were taken, early in the twentieth century.
[2]Open to the public.
[3]Leaseholder.

[2]Open to the public.
[4]Owners at the time photographs were taken.

The Earliest Houses
On Nantucket—1659-1750

The Earliest Houses
On Nantucket—1659-1750

THE first permanent settlers came to Nantucket from Salisbury, Massachusetts, in 1659, and the first houses which they built on the little windswept island were probably crude, temporary huts, providing little more than the proverbial roof over their heads. These early settlers were not destitute. Their expenses were slight; there was food to be had from the sea and land; and as soon as their immediate needs for survival had been provided, they began to build substantial and comfortable homes in the vicinity of Capaum Pond which was then a sheltered harbor connected with the sea. Since at that time the island was under the jurisdiction of New York Province (until it was ceded in 1693 to the Province of Massachusetts by a special act of King William III and Mary), Governor Lovelace gave the name to the township in 1673, calling it Sherburne.

These earliest dwellings, following the general design of those built in the Merrimac Valley in Massachusetts, were imitations of the simple, provincial manor house of late Elizabethan and early Jacobean times in southeast England, adapted to local materials and conditions. Their frames consisted of heavy timbers, hand-hewn and fastened together with pegs in mortise-and-tenon joints. In the earliest house surviving on Nantucket, the outside sheathing boards run vertically and are fastened to the sill and plate with no studs between the posts. An outside covering of shingles was then nailed to the sheathing, and the space between the sheathing and inside plaster was filled with clay for insulation against the bitter winter winds that sweep across the island from the Atlantic.

The rooms, dominated by large fireplaces with cooking ovens set in the back, had low ceilings and were lighted by small wooden casements filled with tiny diamond-shaped pieces of glass. Such casements were used singly or in groups of two or three. There was no attempt to conceal the construction, and the framing projected beyond the inside finished walls into the room. The edges of exposed structural members were often softened to the eye by beading and chamfering, and posts which carried the girts were decorated with shaped tops. The fireplace wall was usually sheathed with wide vertical boards, while the other walls were crudely plastered.

Access to the house was through a heavy batten door into a minute entry leading to a room at one side or to a room on either side. A steep, winding stair ascending against the chimney was all but concealed by wood sheathing in the entry. If more space was required, rooms were added at the rear of the structure and the addition was covered with a shedlike continuation of the steeply pitched main roof, the resulting type of house being called a lean-to.

This plan was very popular, but while it persisted with various modifications until the end of the eighteenth century, Nantucket eventually developed a plan that was indigenous to the island. This will be described in a later section, "The Typical Nantucket House."

Sometime late in the seventeenth or early in the eighteenth century, the entrance of the harbor at Capaum was closed by a severe storm, forming Capaum Pond. This misfortune necessitated the removal of the original settlement to a new site at Wesco on the Great Harbor. The shift was gradual, but by 1720 the town was flourishing in its new location.

It is debatable if trees in any great quantity have ever grown on Nantucket; certainly not a species suitable for house timbers. The earliest dwellings, constructed from lumber laboriously brought from the mainland, were too valuable to be abandoned, and they were either moved or taken down and rebuilt at the new site of the town. Many houses while in the process of being moved were undoubtedly remodeled and enlarged to satisfy the needs of a growing family. Therefore, an older structure may well be hidden under a younger skin, while on the other hand, old timbers, floor boards, doors and windows may be found in a structure of a later date. Because of Nantucket's isolation and the increasing restrictions of the spreading Quaker faith, local customs and conditions changed slowly. Accepted plans and structural details were adhered to by many builders, even while they were incorporating new ideas. Many houses, therefore, have the appearance of being older than they are, with the result that it is often impossible to ascribe to them exact dates.

A gradual transition from the primitive early colonial architecture to what is called the typical Nantucket house occupied the first half of the eighteenth century, coinciding with the Georgian period in England. Basic framing methods continued to be used, but the structural members became less massive. Fireplace openings grew smaller, although the cooking oven was still retained at the back. Window openings became larger and more numerous. The small casement sash was replaced by double-hung sash, composed of twelve over twelve 6″ x 8″ glass panes, set in plank frames that projected beyond the surface of the exterior wall. The upper sash was fixed in the frame. Raised paneling began to be used on fireplace walls instead of the simple, wide vertical boards of earlier interiors. Roofs became less steeply pitched.

Many older houses were renovated during this period. Lean-tos were added at the rear, and the additional space was used for a new kitchen with a fireplace, a small bedroom called a "borning room," a buttery, and an enclosed, winding back stair to the second floor. This new arrangement left the front rooms available for more formal use, and as a consequence the fireplace opening in these rooms was often reduced by building a new fireplace within the old. By the end of the first half of the eighteenth century, it was common to build the rear wall of the house the same height as the front wall. Then, about 1750, was evolved the distinctive Nantucket dwelling which, while keeping many older features, was in its plan a departure from that used earlier in the century.

THE JETHRO COFFIN HOUSE — Sunset Hill

Standing in an open field and surrounded by relatively few buildings, the Jethro Coffin House (also known as the Oldest House and the Horseshoe House) opens its door to visitors during the summer months, and with a stretch of the imagination they may see in the view from its diamond-paned windows a glimpse of the island as it must have looked in the early years of its settlement when there were probably no more than thirty houses on the island.

Tradition says that the house was built in 1686 as a wedding present to Jethro and Mary Coffin from their fathers, Peter Coffin and John Gardner. Its timbers are supposed to have been brought from Exeter, New Hampshire, where Peter Coffin owned large tracts of woodland.

The dwelling, which faces south, is the lean-to type with a massive brick chimney in the center serving four fireplaces. The significance of the horseshoe-shaped figure in brick on the south side of the chimney remains a mystery.

No one knows whether it was originally a symbol to bring good luck or keep away evil spirits or whether it was merely an ornament.

The plank front door, hung on long strap hinges, opens into a tiny entry with a winding stair giving access to the second floor. On either side of the entry is a large room with an enormous fireplace taking up most of one wall. On the second floor are two bedchambers, directly over the two front rooms below, one of which has a smaller fireplace.

The house has no studding, the outside boards being placed vertically and nailed to the sills and girts. Strength is supplied at the corners by braces fastened diagonally between the corner posts and girts. Both oak and pine have been used in the structural timbers, the pine being replacement. Clay has been used as insulation between the outside boarding and the plastered walls.

6

The southwest parlor features a large fire-place with curved sides and a fine gate-leg table.

The kitchen fireplace (*below*) added in 1928 when the Jethro Coffin House was restored.

Before the restoration there was a jog in the lean-to caused by a fire. Sharing the lean-to with the kitchen and buttery is a small "borning room" which also opens into the front parlor.

What came to be known as the kitchen was, in the 1600's, called a hall after the English name for the room where cooking, eating, and much of daily living was carried on. The hall, it may be assumed, was in the southeast room, since the large fireplace has a cooking oven.

(The lean-to, which now contains the kitchen, was a later addition.)

A bed in the front room was common during the winter months, to take advantage of the fireplace. Firewood was scarce and the most had to be made of what was available.

The ship's knee by the door, holding the girts together, was not part of the original structure, but was added when the corner posts had become weakened.

The southwest chamber on the second floor is a good-sized room with one window. The fireplace with a raised hearth has a mantel shaped somewhat like the keel of a ship. The Nantucket Historical Society has not been able, because of a limited budget, to restore the second floor to its original condition, and the wall which has lost some of its plaster gives one a chance to observe the vertical plank construction of the interior partitions. Laths were applied directly to the vertical plank which was about an inch thick, and plaster mixed with hair was applied over the lath.

The closet at the left of this room is known as the Indian Closet from a story which relates that a drunken Indian hid in it and attempted to pursue Mary Coffin when she returned from an errand. When she snatched up her baby and ran out of the house, the Indian, coming to grief on the winding stair, fell and knocked himself unconscious.

THE JOSEPH GARDNER HOUSE

The handsomely restored Joseph Gardner House at 139 Main Street is assumed by some experts to have been built by him sometime in the last quarter of the seventeenth century. Moved to its present location around 1928, it originally faced south as it does now. It is a lean-to type of structure, two stories high in front, with a steeply sloping north roof that sweeps down to one story in the back. The framing is unusual for the island. The corner posts have bracketed tops, not only on the second floor but also on the first floor. The girts and summers have chamfered edges and, being almost a foot square, are unusually heavy.

Joseph Gardner's son, Caleb, eventually took possession of the house when his father moved to another part of the town. For many years before it was moved to its present location, the house was used as a carriage shed and is so remembered by many of the older members of the community today.

The living room or parlor, seen from the front entry, is well furnished with fine old pieces made for the most part in the early eighteenth century. The younger pieces, such as a Sheraton-style sofa under the diamond-paned window, live on friendly terms with the older generation. The door at the left in the far wall was especially put in to exhibit the clay-filled space between the walls. In the fore-ground is a Queen Anne lowboy of high quality.

10

Directly opposite the front door, winding stairs lead to the second floor. Curiously enough, the height of the risers varies considerably from step to step, and without doubt this flight of stairs can be called the most dangerous on the island. Fortunately, a more satisfactory stairway has been provided in another part of the house.

The original chimney, nine feet square at its base, was removed when the structure became a carriage shed. A new chimney, serving three fireplaces, two on the first floor and one on the second, has been designed to duplicate as far as possible the original one. A fine ladder-back armchair stands at the right of the parlor fireplace.

The prototype of the early New England house of this period exists in rural England. The rooms, with raised sill and massive hewn posts, girts and beams, are lighted by small leaded, diamond-paned windows in true medieval fashion. In the dining room, located in an ell with a shed roof to the right of the front entry, a handsome early eighteenth-century armchair with carved arms dominates one corner.

The fireplace is large enough to stand in. In the open door are panes of glass, a variation of a typical Nantucket feature. Harpoon irons hang at the left of the fireplace.

A bedchamber, the same size as the parlor below it, occupies most of the second floor. The posts with bracketed tops and the girts and summers make the exposed framing in the bedchamber a part of the decoration. A soft pink has been chosen for the wall color. At the right of the fireplace, with its raised hearth framed by large quarter-round molding, is an early slant-top desk.

It is usually possible to date a house approximately by the size of its fireplaces, but even in the earliest houses the chamber fireplaces were small, as in this room. Over the fireplace are lithographs by Edgar W. Jenney who has also done a series of water colors of Nantucket interiors which was exhibited at the New York Metropolitan Museum of Art.

The Joseph Gardner House   13

12 LIBERTY STREET

It is possible that the old house on the south-west corner of Liberty Street and Walnut Lane started its existence early in the eighteenth century as a two-room house near Capaum Pond, the first settlement on the island. If so, it is difficult to say just when the house was moved to its present site on land "set off" in 1723 by the Proprietors to Thomas Macy. It is also puzzling why the house faces north, contrary to the custom of this period which took full advantage of sunshine in the principal rooms by facing houses to the south. The house is of the lean-to type, with a small front entry flanked by a room on either side.

The original fireplace was discovered behind two small fireplaces. Eight feet, five inches in width, it has a recess in the back wall below which the bricks are set in the characteristic herringbone pattern.

In the lean-to a long room on the south side, made by removing a partition, is a sitting room where once was a kitchen. The furnishings of this room are an object lesson for the collector of early American antiques. Each item has, as far as possible, been kept in its original state.

Many an important piece of early furniture has been spoiled by the removal of its original finish, but by keeping their furnishings in mint condition, these owners have created an atmosphere of authenticity in harmony with their house.

The fireplace in the lean-to sitting room is given its proper importance by the grouping of furniture and an extensive collection of cooking utensils. A painted pine settle and an early Pilgrim slatback frame the fireplace. The long wooden bracket above the mantel shelf was used for drying and warming blankets.

An example of the careful preservation of a fine piece, the blanket chest standing against the vertical pine sheathing keeps its old red paint. Comfort has been provided with several upholstered chairs covered with appropriate fabrics.

A well-turned, reeded, banister-back chair and a primitive stand with a slanted top made to hold a book are placed before a well-filled bookcase in a corner of the sitting room. An old carpenter's scriber hangs on the wall. Oriental rugs, here as well as in the rest of the house, have been mixed effectively with hooked rugs. Through the doorway is a glimpse of the northwest parlor, and at the extreme right a batten door opens to the back stair.

The northwest bedchamber over the parlor has a fireplace with a raised hearth on which rests a ratchet and pawl candlestand. A mid-eighteenth-century highboy, a late Sheraton chair made early in the nineteenth century, and a pencil-post canopied bed with a linsey-woolsey coverlet are among the furnishings. The door at the right gives access to the lean-to.

The fireplace mantel in the northeast bedchamber is a late one, installed long after the house was built. Two children's chairs stand before the fireplace, the older of the two on the left. The pencil-post bed has a fish-net canopy. Since this picture was taken, the modern floor has been replaced with old, wide pine boards.

THE TOBEY HOUSE

Standing at the intersection of Main, Milk and Gardner streets on Monument Square, one views a cross section of Nantucket architecture dating from the early eighteenth to the late nineteenth century. The oldest structure in the group has been called for many years the Tobey House after Mrs. Benjamin G. Tobey, a granddaughter of Tristram Starbuck, one of the original owners.

The house was ably restored in the nineteen twenties, and with the exception of the famous Three Bricks and the Oldest House on Sunset Hill, is the most photographed house on Nan-

tucket. It is made up of several sections, the oldest of which is said to have been moved from its original site near Capaum Pond. This section, the east one, is probably late seventeenth or early eighteenth century in date, while the west section dates from 1753.

A view from the tiny front entry, looking into the older east section. Ascent up this winding stair has the protection of two types of rope handrails. The two circular windows over the door are an early form of the typical Nantucket "lights" over interior doors.

20   *The Tobey House*

The dining room *(facing page)*, in the western half of the house, is smaller than the room on the east and has a much smaller fireplace. The Sheraton fancy chairs in this room, although almost a century younger than this section of the house, in no way seem out of place. Handsome Canton china platters act as wall decoration.

The east section with its very large fireplace is used as a parlor. The fireplace has an oven at its back, indicating that the room was once a kitchen or "hall." The exposed framing is original with the exception of the sills which have had to be replaced. Sills in the earliest houses were laid directly on the ground and were therefore the first part of the framing to rot.

In the study, in the north side of the lean-to, is another large fireplace with an oven. The batten door in the left foreground opens onto a winding stair to the second floor, a plan typical of this type of house and found in other houses of the same age on the island. On the paneled door leading to the cellar stair, directly to the left of the fireplace, appear a wooden latch (facing page) and a whalebone knob. A latchstring opens this door from the stair side.

MILL HILL

In 1934 Richards Emerson combined two of Nantucket's older houses into a single dwelling on the site of one of the four windmills which once stood on the Popsquatchet Hills, that section of Nantucket now called Mill Hill. Moving an ancient house from New Street and another from upper Main Street, both of which were falling into disrepair, he added old timbers from the Hamblin property on Cliff Road. The result of this reconstruction is a house in the style of the early 1700's. The leaded diamond-paned windows were copied from a casement sash taken from a house on Gull Island, a relic which may still be seen at the Fair Street Museum. The front-door stone, in which are cut the letters "G" and "E," is also from the Hamblin property. Tradition says these are the initials of George Gardner (son of Captain John Gardner) who owned the Cliff Road land, and of Eunice Starbuck whom he married in 1696.

The age of the basic structure may readily be seen in the raised sill, posts with molded brackets, and girts and summers. Crewel curtains reaching to the floor are used at the windows. An early eighteenth-century slat-back armchair stands at the right, close to a tip-top table with Dutch feet.

Many off-island owners become so fond of their Nantucket houses that they reopen them for Thanksgiving. To them, that day in November means "home to the island." Canton china has been used here for the holiday table setting. The head of the family uses a Carver armchair while the other members sit in Hitchcocks.

A skilful reconstruction is the large fireplace with a recessed back and herringbone panel below it. A braced Windsor child's chair of the fanback type stands at the left.

In one corner of the dining room a pine wall cupboard holds a collection of Canton china. Here, too, are clearly visible the raised sill and bracketed corner post. A silver-plated fire horn stands on the floor at the left.

Important in the furnishing of the west bed-chamber is a paneled blanket chest with plain ends and bracket feet. The upholstered chair is a copy of an old Nantucket piece.

Windows in another bedchamber command a fine view of the ocean beyond undulating moors. A richly carved bed with a painted canopy shares attention with a slant-top desk. A Chippendale scroll mirror with applied three-feather crest hangs over the desk.

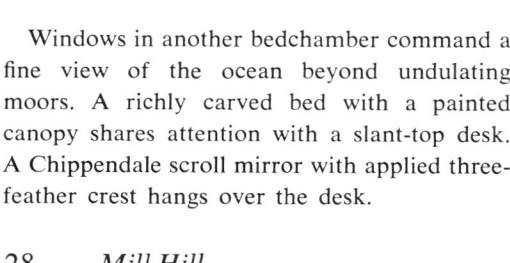

THE RICHARD GARDNER HOUSE

Facing south and overlooking Lily Pond, an early house of the lean-to type turns its back on the main thoroughfare of West Chester Street, one of the oldest streets of Nantucket Town. The house was built early in the eighteenth century for Captain Richard Gardner, whose grandfather was granted, in 1667, the large section of land known as the "Crooked Record" because of its irregular shape. Captain Gardner was eventually lost at sea while on a whaling voyage. Priam Brock, who obtained the house in 1822, met a similar fate although his wife did not learn of his death until two years later. A son, Peter Brock, who had never seen his father, lived in the house until his death in 1908.

The paneling, which was discovered under canvas and wallpaper, is probably a later addition. A base has been painted across the paneling; the edges of the girts and summer are beaded.

In this house the stair with its turned newel post, balusters and molded handrail has received more attention than is usual in this period. Instead of the simple, sharply winding stair behind vertical sheathing, a different arrangement of treads provides a more comfortable ascent to the second floor than is found in the earliest houses. It is possible an older stair wore out and that this stair is a replacement. The "lights," too, are probably a later addition.

The under side of the winding garret stair has been plastered in a smooth curve.

At the top of the garret stair, one has an opportunity to observe the construction of the roof. Purlins cross horizontally from rafter to rafter, and the roof boards have been laid vertically.

An inviting view of the west parlor can be seen from the front entry. A fine reeded banister-back chair is an impo-tant member of a grouping that includes a banjo clock and a lowboy with claw-and-ball feet.

The arrangement on top of the lowboy leaves nothing to be desired. A handsome pewter pitcher holds one of the many varieties of Nantucket's wildflowers. Their suitability as decoration in island interiors is quite evident here. The banjo clock is an excellent one; the candlestick is European.

The transoms or "lights" over interior doors in Nantucket houses have great decorative value. Two variations can be seen in this view of the parlor from the library.

The library, which once was the kitchen, is in the lean-to section of the house. Leather-bound books line the west wall. The gate-leg table is a very early American one; a board connects the trestles and the swinging gate is flat. Important in the furnishings of the room is a slant-front desk with an unusual arrangement of pigeonholes.

The natural wood of the floor is enlivened by colorful Oriental rugs, often more suitable in an old house than braided or hooked rugs. The fireplace, with an oven at the side, was added years after the house was built.

The dining room has the largest fireplace in the house and this one probably once had an oven, as this room was usually the kitchen. A chair-table, called a hutch table, is used for dining. The chairs are Hitchcock. A hanging candelabrum, although not old, is in keeping with the room.

The bedchamber fireplace has built above it a cupboard with very old, irregular glass in its door. A child's chair with unusual turnings and a Windsor with bamboo turnings are used on either side of the fireplace which is still giving service.

The Richard Gardner House   35

153 MAIN STREET

One of Nantucket's earlier houses stands at
153 Main Street. Built sometime early in the
eighteenth century, it was first owned by Barnabas Gardner. It passed from the Gardner family, in 1804, to Benjamin Whippey who in
turn conveyed it to Alfred Folger in 1821. For
many years it was known as the Folger House.

The house, a two-story lean-to, faces south.
The room to the right of the entry is the "hall"
in which the family spent most of the daylight
hours, and here they cooked and ate before its
large fireplace.

The room at the left of the entry was the
parlor, used for formal occasions and for re-
ceiving visitors. A four-post bedstead was cus-
tomarily kept in this room.

Upstairs, the parlor chamber over the parlor
was the parents' bedroom. The children were
consigned to the hall chamber where there was
always an assortment of beds. If the brood was
a large one, the overflow was taken care of in
the garret.

The "hall" is now used as the parlor, and has lost its large fireplace with a cooking oven at the back. Replacing it is a smaller fireplace and a paneled wall finished in natural wood. Rockers have been added to the Windsor armchair with bamboo turnings. Next to it a small tavern table of early eighteenth-century date holds a product for which Nantucket is famous — the Nantucket lightship basket.

In this exceptional grouping of furniture, the center of attraction is the armchair with Flemish back and carved arms. Two early eighteenth-century stands, one with a tripod base, the other with a "T" base, occupy convenient places by the chair and sofa.

153 Main Street   37

The massive construction of the house is visible in the parlor. Through the back of a Windsor chair can be glimpsed an early eighteenth-century, transitional slat-back armchair, unusual in that it shows the influence of a Carver chair by the use of a top rail over the slats. The other Windsor armchair in front of the mid-eighteenth-century desk is exceptional in design. A Nantucket lightship basket is used as a wastebasket.

A view of the same room from the front entry. At the right a paneled mirror board has replaced the post under the molded bracket carrying the summer. This replacement was probably a late eighteenth-century change.

38   *153 Main Street*

The back room, once used as a kitchen, has been made into a living room. The ceiling in this room was very low, and therefore the floor was lowered when the house was remodeled. The room was also enlarged by the removal of a partition.

The room which was used as a parlor in the early days of the house is now a bedroom. The doorway at the left leads to the front entry.

This rare blanket chest in the living room *(facing page)* is a very early one, made at the end of the seventeenth or beginning of the eighteenth century. The pair of mirrors are Vauxhall glass; the box is Chinese.

The mantel in this bedchamber is not the original one. Mantels are generally an indication of late eighteenth-century work. The small cupboard high in the wall is sometimes known as a "parson's cupboard."

A mushroom slat-back armchair and a modern upholstered armchair have been used on either side of the fireplace.

QUARTER MILE HILL

Facing south in an open field on Quarter Mile Hill, stands an early house moved there some years ago from Main Street. The main section of the house, built in the second quarter of the eighteenth century, consisted of a one-sided, two-story lean-to with the usual tiny front entry and simple winding stair to the second floor. At the right of the entry was a single room with a corresponding room above, and there was an additional room in the lean-to. At some time during the second half of the eighteenth century, a one-story ell with a shed roof was added, providing a room to the left of the entry. The large wing on the east side and the dormers are fairly recent additions. The whole is an interesting example of the changes made in an old house during its long lifetime, changes which in this case have increased its livability without affecting its charm.

In the upstairs hall an ancient batten door closes off the garret. A smooth curve of plaster ceiling is applied directly to the under side of the garret stair.

42

The age of many an old house can be determined not only by the size of its fireplaces but also by the design of the front entry. The stair in this house is the original one, and its simplicity indicates an early eighteenth-century construction.

The room in the one-story ell is now a living room with an unusual cupboard built into one of its corners. A painted baseboard has been carried across the vertical sheathing. A pair of transition Dutch chairs with Spanish feet stand on either side of a Chippendale table with square fluted legs.

The size of the fireplace in the living room has probably been reduced and the paneling with an arch over the opening added at a later date, for this arch is a unique treatment of the fireplace on Nantucket.

What is now the study was once a kitchen, for it has a fireplace and a cooking oven in the wall beside it. This arrangement is a late eighteenth-century design. Probably a larger fireplace with an oven at its back occupied this space when the house was first built.

The paneling in the dining room suggests that it was also a later addition around a reduced fireplace opening. The original fireplace was much larger, occupying most of the area now covered by raised paneling. The change was probably made late in the eighteenth century.

21 MILK STREET

On the northeast corner of Milk Street and Copper Lane is a house which may be considered a transitional design between the lean-to and the typical Nantucket styles. In it the lean-to has been given up and the rear is two stories high. The arrangement of small entry with winding stair against the chimney and one room on either side has still been used, but the rooms are of different size, foreshadowing the off-center house that was to be built in such quantities later in the eighteenth century.

The land it occupies is in that old part of Nantucket known as Chicken Hill. The lot is unusually large for a Nantucket house, and on the east side contains some fine old box bushes.

The massive fireplace of the earlier house has been replaced by a smaller fireplace and a paneled wall. A wrought-iron floor candlestand with brass finial and drip saucers stands at the left of the fireplace.

A wooden sea chest with beckets has been used against the paneled cradle board. The chair in front of it is an early version of the Salem rocker and was made on the island.

In this house the kitchen has always been in the rear. On the evidence of the size of the fireplace opening, for these became smaller during the eighteenth century, and the fact that the oven with an iron door is still at the back of the fireplace, not at the side as was common at the end of the century, the construction of the house may be set in the 1740's or 1750's.

The kitchen, now used as a living-kitchen, was once three rooms. Partitions dividing off the "borning room" and buttery have been removed, making one large room. A back stair to the second floor is accessible from this room. In general, the plan remains that of the earlier lean-to.

THE SARA TURNER HOUSE

An old photograph of the house at 86 Center Street, long known as the Sara Turner House, shows the original structure before additions were made. The house, a one-and-a-half-story lean-to facing south, is a smaller version of the two-story lean-to. It was built in the mid-1700's when it was customary to place the kitchen in the lean-to.

The parlor on the southeast side has a fireplace in a fine paneled wall. The kitten playing with a wool ball on the hooked rug is a Victorian idea of fun cast in iron. The chairs on either side of the fireplace are also Victorian.

The passway between the dining room and parlor was once the front entry, with the usual winding stair against the large central chimney.

Visible at the right is the paneled fireplace wall. At the left the parlor extends beyond what was originally the front of the house.

The dining room was probably originally used as a bedchamber. Except in the earliest houses, brick is rarely used as facing for Nantucket fireplace openings, cement-plaster being the usual material which in this dining room has been painted black. The paneled fireplace walls in both the dining room and parlor have been scraped of former coats of paint. The large panels on the right are over twenty-four inches wide.

The Sara Turner House   51

The breakfast area, part of the kitchen, is a fairly recent addition, blending successfully with the older part of the house. Both walls and ceiling have been papered. The room was pleasantly dappled with sunshine on the warm October day when this picture was taken, and a most obliging cat took charge of the foreground.

Another view of the kitchen and breakfast area shows how it is possible to create a compatible atmosphere in an old house without limiting oneself to an accepted formula.

52   *The Sara Turner House*

PARLIAMENT HOUSE

The house on the northeast corner of Pine and School streets has long been known as Parliament House. It consists of two different structures built a century apart. The north section, the older of the two, is supposed to have been built on the hill northwest of Hummock Pond and to have been the home of Nathaniel Starbuck and his wife, Mary, who figures prominently in the Quaker movement on Nantucket. Seventh child of one of the original settlers, Tristram Coffin, she became a celebrated preacher. Meetings were held in her home and the house became known as Parliament House, presumably because it had a room big enough for large gatherings. There is some doubt, however, whether the Parliament House mentioned in town records and the present house at 10 Pine Street are the same.

The north section is supposed to have been moved to its present site in 1820 by John Folger, who also at that time added the south section.

The parlor in the south section has an early nineteenth-century mantel. The passway at the right, made possible by a jog in the chimney, leads to a back parlor.

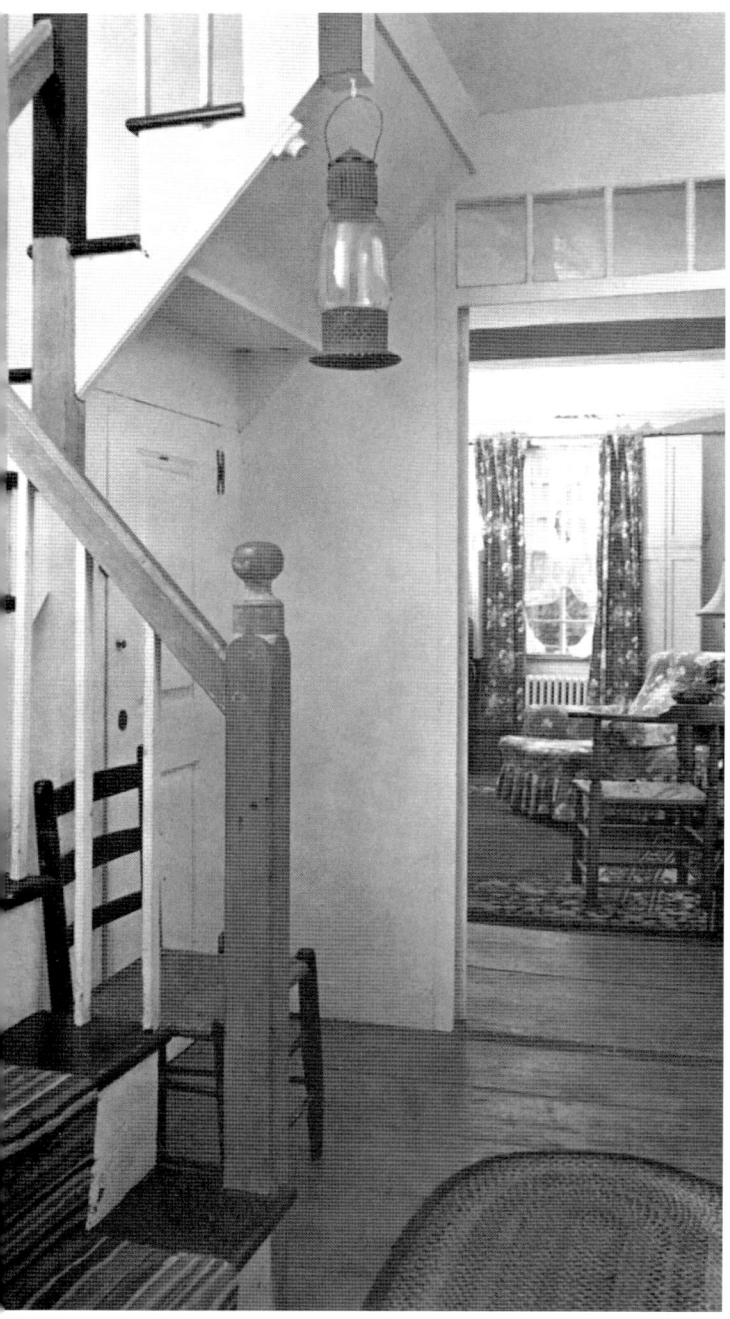 

The turning that crowns the plain, square newel post is the only attempt at decoration in the front entry and assumes importance amid the simplicity of the other components. The parlor can be glimpsed through the open door.

A tinsmith who once lived in Parliament House fashioned the narrow tin frame for the hinged pane in the "lights" over the door. The crookedness of most Nantucket floors is responsible for the prop under the chest-on-chest.

54   *Parliament House*

The Nantucket closet is unusually large and is equipped with wide shelves let into the plaster wall. A closet window is customary, and the size and arrangement of four panes over four of this one date this as early eighteenth-century, a clue to the age of the older section of Parliament House.

The panel molding on the dining room door is unusual in that it has an additional quarter-round bead. (For the usual molding, see page 23.) Marks left by the hand plane are still apparent on the door. When scraping paint off old woodwork, it is desirable to leave such evidence of hand planing as well as any scratches acquired through the years which, like wrinkles in an old face, show character. These prove the capacity of old houses to grow old gracefully.

Parliament House 55

A view on the second floor, looking into the older section of Parliament House. A small fireplace has been tucked into a corner of the bedchamber. "Lights" over a two-paneled door, a four-over-four-paned window, and simple painted sheathing are all elements which go into making an old Nantucket interior.

56   *Parliament House*

THE JOSHUA COFFIN HOUSE

The entrance with sidelights of the Joshua Coffin House at 52 Center Street is not the original one, being typical of early nineteenth-century design.

The beam in the front entry is a clue for an approximate dating of the house in the 1750's. The stair is obviously the work of a local car-penter, equipped with crude tools but creating with them a graceful, if naive design. The door is of a later period.

Hanging strips were used extensively in Nantucket halls, closets and bedrooms. This one is in a closet on the second floor.

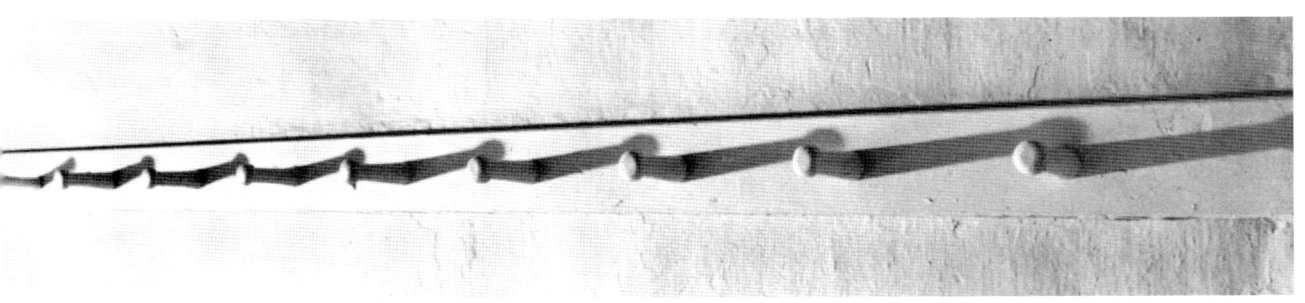

Children growing up in the Joshua Coffin House must have had a delightful time, for here is a secret room built into the heart of the massive central chimney. It is reached through a concealed trap door in the floor of the garret and lighted by an interior window let into the wall of the front entry. The window is in all probability a later addition. No one knows what the secret room was used for, but at the time of the Revolutionary War and again during the War of 1812, Nantucket was subjected to British invasion and a secret room such as this would have been extremely useful during those trying times.

58   *The Joshua Coffin House*

33 ORANGE STREET

The little house at 33 Orange Street has the distinction of being the home of Nantucket's beloved Dr. Will Gardner, author of a number of informative books on Nantucket's past. The house was built in 1760 by a Wyer and inherited by his son, Christopher, a whaling master. At one time the house was owned by the first Unitarian minister on the island, Seth Swift.

Structurally the house is a one-sided lean-to, a term indicating that the entry has only one room at its side. In this case the stair is not placed against the chimney but against the outside wall. Double protection for a safe descent is provided by a wooden handrail and a knotted rope hung from the head of the stair.

The paneled wall in the parlor and the bolection molding with crossetted corners around the fireplace are later additions. A larger, original fireplace still exists behind the one visible here. Fireplace openings on Nantucket were usually larger than those on the mainland, even in early nineteenth-century houses.

111 MAIN STREET

The house at 111 Main Street has had a varied history. It was built by Ebenezer Gardner as a wedding present for his daughter, Margaret, when she married Captain Daggett. In 1787 it was owned by Barnabas Macy, whose heirs, when he died, transferred it to the Nantucket Monthly Meeting of Friends. The building became a home for aged and needy Quakers and from 1827 to 1882 was known as The Friends' Boarding House.

Originally the structure was of the lean-to type, but early in the nineteenth century a section of the rear was removed and another

house attached. As a result, the house has two central chimneys serving nine fireplaces. Both inside and out the house has been considerably remodeled and looks younger than it actually is. Much of the renovating was done at the time the house was owned by the Society of Friends.

A view of the rear of the house shows how houses grow on Nantucket. Lean-tos with various sizes of windows are casually added to an existing house, but ivy and climbing roses blend confusion together into a whole.

In the dining room, over the arrangement of Sandwich glass in the bellflower pattern, hangs a late eighteenth-century mirror with carved urn and wired grasses.

The two front rooms on either side of the front entry are unusually large and the furniture they contain is of fine quality. The present owner has specialized in a fine collection of chairs. From this parlor a doorway leads to the dining room in back.

The present dining room was probably once the kitchen with a fireplace on the opposite side of the room. The present fireplace was installed when the house was added to early in the nineteenth century.

A fine Hepplewhite side chair with spade feet stands at the left of the fireplace. A primitive corner cabinet displays a tea set of strawberry luster and a collection of Wedgewood. The tip-and-turn tripod table at the right of the cabinet has a mechanical device at the top

of the shaft called a crow's nest. Also sometimes called a bird cage, it is made up of a turning square with four posts at the corners, topped with another square on which the circular top is hinged.

A large collection of Sandwich glass in the bellflower pattern (*facing page*) is an important part of the decoration in the dining room. Practically every piece made in this pattern is represented in the collection.

12 ORANGE STREET

This grouping of furniture might well be called "The Story Hour." The upholstered wing chair is an early eighteenth-century piece which belonged to the Swain ancestress whose portrait *(facing page)* hangs in the same room. All the children's chairs are nineteenth century.

The house is much older than the early nine-teenth-century mantel would have one believe, having been built in the mid-1700's. The two-panel door at the right opens to a long, narrow passage between the winding front stair and the large central chimney and gives access to the other side of the house without going through the second-floor entry.

Two fine oil portraits painted by William Swain in 1843 hang in the parlor. The painter was a Nantucket artist and these portraits were done after he had studied in Europe. The subjects, Mr. and Mrs. Benjamin Tucker, were Nantucket Quakers. Much of the furniture in the room belonged to them. Mrs. Tucker was the sister of Margaret Swain, the great-great-grandmother of the present owner of the house.

25 PLEASANT STREET

At the old house at 25 Pleasant Street lived the parents of Cyrus Hussey, crew member of the ship "Globe" on which, in 1824, took place one of the bloodiest mutinies ever to occur on a whaler. The ringleader, Samuel Comstock, practically singlehanded killed the captain, Thomas Worth, and three officers, after which deed the mutineers proceeded to sail the ship to the Mulgrave Islands in the Eastern Marshalls. There, one night, five of the crew who had taken no part in the mutiny escaped with the ship, while the rest of the mutineers were left on shore, two innocent young shipmates, Cyrus Hussey and Thomas Lay, with them. Trouble soon ensued between the mutineers and the natives, in the course of which all the white men except Hussey and Lay were killed. The natives held the two youths in captivity during which they were tattooed from head to foot, until they were rescued by the schooner "Dolphin" of the United States Navy, commanded by Captain John Percival. The boys returned to Nantucket where they wrote an account of the mutiny, and eventually shipped aboard whaleships and were never heard of in Nantucket again.

It is known that in 1745 the Hussey dwelling was a lean-to in its present location, and therefore the date of its construction can be assumed to be in the second quarter of the eighteenth century. A partition has been removed between the east parlor and a small room in the lean-to, resulting in a long living room. Plaster walls, painted white, contrast with gray-blue painted woodwork.

The house, facing south with its side on Pleasant Street, is entered through a box garden. The small entry leads to a parlor on the right and a dining room on the left which may be glimpsed in this view. The stair to the bedchambers on the second floor is a departure from the usual winding stair in a house of this period.

A sofa in Chippendale style, placed at right angles to the paneled fireplace wall, is covered with a blue fabric. It lies along the line of a former partition removed to enlarge the parlor. The chair at the right in front of the grandfather clock is a transitional Queen Anne piece.

Windows of three different sizes light the parlor, those on the front being the widest. Double shutters, hinged at one side, afford protection on a cold blustery night. The Sheraton Martha Washington chair at the left is covered in the same fabric as that used for the curtains. The high-backed armchair, covered in a rough off-white cotton, is Queen Anne in style.

On the second floor the east bedchamber has white plaster walls and the woodwork is painted a soft shade of tan, the fabric at the windows and in the canopy picking up both these colors in its design. Hanging over the Franklin fire-frame is a portrait of George Washington, who did not sleep here. The door at the left of the Sheraton gilt mirror opens to a room in the lean-to.

Cyrus Hussey probably often thought long-ingly about this bedchamber with its com-fortable bed and fireplace during his two-year stay with the natives in the Mulgraves. Inserted high in the plastered fireplace wall are curious wooden, diamond-shaped inserts which formerly had pegs on which damp clothes were dried. In many Nantucket bedchambers there is instead a peg strip over the fireplace.

THE JOHN SWAIN HOUSE

On a slight rise back from Polpis Road, where one can look across the moors to the Upper Harbor, stands a reconstruction of the John Swain House. The original house was destroyed by lightning in August, 1902, after a life of over two centuries, and the island lost one of its oldest houses. In the reconstruction a modified plan of the original was followed. The oldest part of the building was the central section, and the west end was built around 1800.

70

THE 1735 HOUSE

One of the earliest houses on Union Street, Number 22 has undergone many vicissitudes. Known at one time as the old Hezekiah Broadbrook Place, it was rescued from falling into ruins in the late 1920's and made into a restaurant called The Chopping Bowl. On the death of the proprietor, the house was again neglected and rescued anew by the present owner. Although it is now called The 1735 House, it is difficult to assign to it an exact date, a problem with many Nantucket houses. In its present location the dwelling faces north. A vestibule has been added, making a larger entry, and on either side of the entry is a room with corresponding rooms on the second floor. This is a view of the entry from the parlor.

71

The Typical Nantucket House

The Typical
Nantucket House

BY the end of the eighteenth century, the gradual shift of population from the neighborhood of Capaum Pond eastward to the present site on Great Harbor had been accomplished. In 1795 the name of the town was changed from Sherburne to Nantucket. At this time Quaker influence, which had been growing since the first Society of Friends was formed in 1708, reached its height, and over half the town's population of nearly five thousand were members of the sect during the period when most of the characteristically Quaker houses were built.

The Quaker faith had great influence on the manners, customs and architecture of Nantucket. Since ostentation was firmly discouraged by those of strict faith, this restriction is evident in the limitation of house decoration during the period to what is generally utilitarian. The exterior and interior character of houses, as well as the dress and manners of people, followed a rigid pattern which eliminated any frustrating effort to keep up with one's neighbors. One significant fact, however, should be noted: the Quaker was an efficient businessman and felt no restriction in his religion to prevent his earning a good living and providing for the future. The quality of his furniture, silver and clothing was always the best he could afford.

The house which his taste evolved on Nantucket stands with quiet, homely dignity close to the public thoroughfare and to its neighbors on either side, leaving an ample backyard to provide a privacy equal to that of a modern well-planned community. The women, who were left alone in these houses when their husbands were at sea, took great comfort in the proximity to each other and to the street where it was possible to watch "the pass" from the front windows.

The typical house is a two-story structure capped with a pitched roof. Often a one-story or two-story ell has been built onto the back as a later addition and a "wart" with a shed roof added at the side. The shingled walls are usually left to weather, their color varying with the weather. After a driving northeaster they are almost black, and when they have been dried by the sun, they become a soft, silvery gray. The trim is usually painted, although the present habit of painting the trim white is a fairly modern innovation. Originally the trim was a dull red or was often left to weather like the shingles.

The earlier version of the Nantucket house is usually built on a low stone foundation, with most of the area under the house unexcavated except for a small, bricked, cylindrical cellar under the kitchen, used for storing vegetables. This version has minor differences from the later version that was built high off the ground on a brick foundation, providing a well-lighted summer kitchen with fireplace and baking oven in the basement.

The front entrance, placed off center, has two windows lighting the parlor on one side and one window lighting a closet on the other. The entrance, as originally built, was merely a projected plank frame similar to that of the windows, with a raised-panel door and "lights" or a transom above it. The more elaborate front-door frames with heavy pilasters and cornices, often seen on this type of house, are usually later additions replacing the original frame at a time when the Quaker influence was beginning to wane and the Greek Revival style was being introduced from the mainland.

The windows have panes of 7″ x 9″ glass, and in the principal rooms each sash is made up of twelve lights, forming a twenty-four-light, double-hung window, sometimes gruesomely known as a "guillotine" window. Windows in the closets and second-floor hall are made of two nine-light sash, forming a window of eighteen lights. The top sash in all cases is fixed.

The diminutive front entry of earlier houses, with its steep stair ascending against the chimney to the second floor, has been replaced by a long, narrow entry and a more elaborate stair with a straight run, winding at the top. A steep, winding stair is used as the back stair. A large well-lighted closet with an eighteen-light window opens off the entry. Light for the entry is furnished through "lights" not only over the front exterior door but over the interior doors as well, letting in illumination from the main rooms of the house.

"Lights" over interior doors are a dominant feature of Nantucket dwellings and are not found in like quantity in any other regional architecture on the mainland. In the earliest houses they were often in the doors themselves. A number of explanations for this feature has been advanced, one being that they were intended to help the occupants to keep an eye on fires in the fireplaces of other rooms. Another explanation, a religious one, suggests that the danger of complete privacy in any room was avoided in this way. It is interesting to note that no "lights" are found over closet doors, even when the additional illumination would have been useful in lighting the entry. The logical explanation, however, seems to be that the "lights" were used for the simple purpose of providing light.

On the first floor the front parlor, accessible from the front entry, has simple restrained paneling on the fireplace wall and a paneled wainscoting, called a "cradle board," on the partition wall. Between the two front windows is a mirror board, which in older houses is only a narrow strip with beaded edges. In later houses this area is apt to be paneled. A simple molded cornice is used at the ceiling in this room. All is put together in the workmanlike manner of the early carpenter who had the time and inclination to do things right.

The kitchen at the back of the house, also accessible from the front entry, had a cooking oven at the side of the fireplace; but after the invention of the cook stove, the oven was often converted into a useful closet for storing wood when the kitchen was moved to a new ell in the rear. The earliest versions of this type of house contain a smaller form of the huge, early colonial fireplace with the cooking oven at its back. As in the earliest houses, the kitchen served also as a dining room and an informal sitting room. It generally had two closets, one under the front stair and a larger one, used as a buttery, with an eighteen-light window behind the closet off the front entry. The third room at the back on the first floor was commonly used as a bedchamber.

The arrangement of rooms on the second floor is similar to that on the first floor. Here are three bedchambers, the front one over the parlor being finished with paneling very much like the parlor. A possible explanation for this paneled upstairs front room may be found in St. John de Crèvecoeur's *Letters from an American Farmer,* where in speaking of Martha's Vineyard he says, "All the houses are neat, convenient and comfortable, some of them filled with two families for when their husbands are at sea, the wives require less houseroom. . . ." This second-floor front room was probably a parlor for the additional family.

Mantels framing the fireplace opening were not used in earlier Quaker houses of this period, and the presence of one indicates a house of nineteenth-century construction or a renovation of an eighteenth-century one. Often a slight effort was made to accent the fireplace opening by painting a dark border around the opening. This painted band was actually a continuation of the painted base board which was carried even across the bottom of doors. Effective as they are, the use of such painted bands cannot be called an attempt at decoration, for they are primarily useful in keeping hidden the marks that were unavoidably made in the daily process of cleaning.

The third floor or garret, made possible by the pitched roof and reached by the back stair, often has one room finished in plaster and lighted by a single window. Except for this finished room, usually used as an additional bedchamber, the rest of the garret was left with the roof construction exposed, even though one had to go through it to reach the bedchamber. In the garret is visible the large chimney, containing the six flues which serve six fireplaces in the rooms below. Here also may be found a steep ladder leading to a hatchway in the roof near the chimney by which one reached the "walk," a popular feature on Nantucket roofs, enabling one to scan the harbor and horizon for incoming and outgoing ships.

The woodwork in this typical house was painted in soft shades, and the resulting effect of lightness subtly expressed the basic idea of the Quaker faith, Inner Light. Today's practice of stripping the paint off the wide pine floor boards, sheathing and paneling in this type of house, while very attractive, does not give an accurate picture of the original interior.

There are subtle variations, in spite of similar plans and details, that keep the typical Nantucket house from row-house monotony. These variations are more easily explained by the photographs that follow.

THE JOB MACY HOUSE

Many an old house that has fallen into disrepair over the years has had the good fortune to be reclaimed by an interested purchaser from off the island. An exceptionally fortunate house is the Job Macy House at 11 Mill Street, facing south on the northwest corner at the intersection of New Dollar Lane, formerly Risdale Street. On an excellently landscaped lot, it has been sympathetically restored inside and out.

The house is said to have been built in the 1750's, a dating substantiated by details of the framing. Legend relates that the builder, Job Macy, incurred the wrath of his father who refused ever to enter the house since it had been built with two stories in front and rear instead

of with a characteristic lean-to under a long, sloping roof in the rear. Anyone entering this attractive house can see that Job's father cut off his nose to spite his face.

The ell was added in 1832 when a master mariner, Joshua Coffin, bought the property. The house is one of the earlier examples of the truly typical Nantucket dwelling. Exterior views before *(right)* and after *(left)* restoration have been included to encourage prospective buyers of old houses who may be timid. Often such neglected houses look forlorn and hopeless; but if they are given understanding treatment, they can be restored to useful and beautiful lives.

The front door opens into a typically long and narrow entry with closets on the outside wall. It is simply furnished with a tall pine-cased clock made by Silas Hoadley of Plymouth, Connecticut, and a mid-eighteenth-century country Queen Anne side chair. The woodwork framing white walls is painted green. Under the peg strip is an old crock holding a collection of whalebone- and ivory-headed canes.

The front parlor was not entirely furnished when these photographs were taken, for the house had been newly acquired. Nevertheless, one sees an indication of the appropriate furnishings to come. Simple white cotton curtains hang at the windows and are uniform all over the house. In front of the window stands a Queen Anne chair with a bold cabriole leg, ending in a claw-and-ball foot. On the Pembroke table under the mid-eighteenth-century mirror in Chippendale style is a Crown Derby bowl flanked by two brass candlesticks.

Other clues to the age of the house can be seen in the exposed framing and the low ceilings. In the later development of this type of house, the ceilings are usually eight feet high on the first floor, and the girt and summer construction is concealed between the first floor ceiling and the second floor by a simple molded cornice at the intersection of wall and ceiling.

The walls throughout the house are white. The woodwork in this room, with the exception of the floor which has been scraped to the natural pine, is painted a soft gray-blue.

The furniture assembled for the dining room includes a matched set of English chairs. This room, surprisingly, also functions as the kitchen which it was originally. A stove, refrigerator, dishwasher, and sink have been concealed in pine cabinets and their modernity is exposed only when they are in use. A deep red paint has been used on the woodwork. Old colors found under later coats of paint throughout the house have been used in other rooms.

The Job Macy House   81

The position of the back stair is still another clue to the age of the house. Although the direction of the ridgepole has been changed, the stair bears practically the same relation to the kitchen fireplace as does the back stair in the earlier lean-to type of house.

Behind the batten door, on the second floor landing, another flight of stairs directly over the back stair leads to the garret.

A partial view of the east back chamber shows a simple bed covered with a patchwork quilt. The under side of the top of the garret stair can be seen above the door.

The front chamber over the parlor has as a focal point a pencil-post bed draped with Bemis bag cloth (a very useful material for creating an authentic atmosphere) and covered with a quilt of linsey-woolsey.

The former kitchen, built in the 1830's by Joshua Coffin, has been made into a large living room. The stair was taken from the garret where formerly it gave access to a "walk" on the roof, reached through a skylight.

The Job Macy House   83

THE JESSE COFFIN HOUSE

This house at 102 Main Street belies its true age. Built in the middle of the eighteenth century, it has undergone such extensive alterations that its early date is shown only in points of construction. The heavy Greek Revival entrance was added in the 1830's when whaling was at its height and successful whaling men wished to keep up with the fashion of the day.

A comparison of the modern window frames here with the projected plank frames of the Maria Mitchell House at 1 Vestal Street (page 90) will show the importance of reproducing the plank frame when restoring an old house of this type, for it is window frames of the older type which cast those shadows on the gray shingled walls that give an old house its individuality.

The rear stair to the second floor shows some of the massive construction of the house. A nautical note is provided by the rope handrail held in place with a "Turk's head" knot.

84

The paneled fireplace wall in the study, while a typical Nantucket feature, is a later renovation. This room was probably once used as a kitchen and had a large fireplace with a cooking oven similar to the one in the Job Macy House.

11 MILK STREET

Joseph Starbuck, who built the Three Bricks on Main Street, was born in the house that stands on the north side of the junction of Milk and New Mill streets. This is another in that group of houses said to have been moved from Sherburne, the site of the first settlement near Capaum Pond. The Starbuck clan was once concentrated around the present location.

The room now used as a dining room was formerly the kitchen. A fireplace of this size is unusual in a typical off-center design of the late eighteenth century and indicates that the house has been remodeled during its long life. The presence of two ovens suggests that the fireplace may have been enlarged. Also, the absence of the usual back stairway in the entry to the left side of the chimney leads one to suspect that its space was incorporated into the present fireplace.

A view of the back passway leading to the former kitchen from the small chamber where Joseph Starbuck was born. A graceful shelf bracket is silhouetted against the light. *Right*, a detail of the "light" over the door between the former kitchen and the front entry.

10 GARDNER STREET

The house at 10 Gardner Street was built by Richard Macy and is now owned by a descendant of Maria Mitchell, the astronomer. It originally stood near Crooked or Long Lane on Duke Street, one of the early roads leading from the original location of the town eastward to Great Harbor. Before the removal of the town to Wesco, Duke Street had many houses on both sides, but now, with the exception of the Elihu Coleman House, not one remains. This house was moved to its present location in 1771.

An early nineteenth-century mantel has replaced the paneling commonly found on the fireplace wall. The oil portrait is of William Mitchell, father of Maria.

Courtesy of Popular Photography

A record of the footsteps of many generations has been worn into the back stair of the house. This type of stair, with treads let into the plaster wall and without a skirt board, is a typical feature in Nantucket houses of this period.

Before it was moved the house probably rested on a low stone foundation, but in its new location it has been placed high off the ground. This change has made possible, in the basement, a summer kitchen with a fireplace and cooking oven at its side, a late eighteenth-century arrangement. Exposed framing affords a view of the hearth construction for the dining room fireplace above.

On the first floor a shed-roofed ell enlarges a bedchamber behind the parlor. This addition is also a Nantucket innovation found on many of the houses of this period. There is a cupboard over the unadorned fireplace opening. The document at the right is a Pennsylvania Dutch Fractur baptismal certificate.

10 Gardner Street   89

THE MARIA MITCHELL HOUSE —
The Typical Nantucket House

Walking west on Vestal Street away from Milk Street, one comes to the Maria Mitchell House at 1 Vestal Street where lived the woman astronomer who discovered a comet. The house was built by Hezekiah Swain and his brother in 1790 and came into the possession of the Mitchell family in 1816 when Aaron Mitchell bought it from Simeon Gardner. In January, 1818, it was sold to a cousin, William Mitchell, and here his daughter, Maria, was born on August 1st of that same year. Later, William sold the property to his brother, Peleg Mitchell, Jr., who around 1850 built the addition on the northwest side of the old kitchen. The dwelling, which is open to the public, is an excellent example of the typical Nantucket house (see Appendix, p. 214).

90

The front door opens into a narrow entry
leading to what was originally the kitchen
directly ahead. This view of the entry was taken
from the kitchen doorway. The door at the
right opens to a flight of stairs leading to a
small storage cellar under the southwest corner
of the house. The cellar is constructed of two
outer stone walls and a semicircular brick interior wall.

The Maria Mitchell House   91

Throwing the entry and entry closet together by removing the partition for extra light and space is one of the most common alterations to which this type of Nantucket house is subject. The change in this house probably antedates William Mitchell's ownership. Such alterations were usually discussed, and there survives here no recollection or tradition of such an alteration; however, evidence of the change exists in the narrow board which replaced the former threshold. In the resulting alcove stands Maria Mitchell's brass telescope on an early nineteenth-century stand. On the floor are two Mitchell fire buckets.

A glimpse of the front parlor from the front entry. On the wall is a quotation from Thoreau's *A Week on the Concord and Merrimack Rivers*, appropriate to the birthplace of the famous woman astronomer: "If there is nothing new on earth, still the traveler always has a resource in the skies. They are constantly turning a new page to view. The wind sets the type on this blue ground, and the inquiring may always read a new truth there."

On sunny days the parlor is bright with light. Solid, two-fold, hinged inside shutters are later additions. Over the tambour desk, of about the same age as the house, is an oil painting of William Mitchell and his daughter Maria at an astronomical problem. In front of the window stands a Queen Anne chair; between the windows is a table of the simple Hepplewhite type. The floor in this room is painted and spattered.

The Maria Mitchell House 93

There is more decoration in the parlor than in the rest of the house. The molding around the fireplace opening is a very simple, shallow bolection. On either side of the fireplace two standards in Sheraton style carry terrestrial and celestial globes.

The window casing or architrave continues completely around the opening instead of stopping at the window stool. The board between the windows, called a mirror board, is usually found in this particular spot, or the space may be paneled. Decorative knobs were screwed into it to help support the hanging mirror.

Left, the stair in the front entry.

Upon entering the "new" kitchen one is swept backward in time, for here are preserved the antique cooking utensils used by another generation as well as the iron pump and sink. As there was formerly in the old kitchen, there is a fireplace furnished with a crane, pothooks and trammels. In Maria Mitchell's time, meals were cooked over the open fire during the spring, autumn and winter months. The door leads to the small summer kitchen built by Peleg Mitchell after he bought the house from William.

The Maria Mitchell House   95

William Mitchell added to the house the ell containing a larger kitchen and a new back stairway. He then removed the original back stair which, curiously enough, ran parallel to the front stair, building in its place a clothes-press on the second floor and a long china closet on the first floor. The old kitchen was transformed into a sitting room, and later into a dining room, after the sink had been moved into the new kitchen. The graining on the new kitchen still covers the doors, mantelpiece, and all plaster and woodwork, even the pump, and extends over the garret stair and skirting board as far as these are visible from the kitchen.

The tiny closet at the front of the house off the upstairs hall became a study for Maria Mitchell, probably the smallest study anyone has ever had. It is well lighted by a large eighteen-light window.

There is a shelf for books, a drawer for writing materials, and a top on which to write — actually a desk one can sit *in*. What more does one really need for the serious study of the heavens?

The Maria Mitchell House   97

The middle back chamber on the second floor. The door leads to a passway into the front chamber and the passway closet, backing up to the large center chimney. Clothes in daily use were hung in this passway on wooden knobs or wrought-iron nails mounted on wooden hanging strips. Necessary in bedrooms in Maria Mitchell's time was the washstand with its basin and bowl and a wooden towel rack. To protect the wall a piece of cloth, called a "splasher," was tacked behind the washstand.

There are only two transoms in the whole Maria Mitchell House. As transoms, or "lights," were the rule in a house of this type, it is safe to assume that earlier transoms have been removed.

The chamber over the front parlor is furnished with pieces from Maria Mitchell's time. The plain muslin window curtains are especially suitable here. Tiebacks are held in place with wrought-iron nails. So-called "ruffled" curtains are a modern innovation and inappropriate to a house of this type.

The Maria Mitchell House   99

In the "Star Chamber" (so named from the stars on its wallpaper), the hanging strip illustrates how utilitarian was the Quaker house. Such strips were used on the fireplace wall in secondary bedchambers as well as in the passway and front entry.

Rooms in houses of this period are unusually well lighted and airy. First-floor ceilings are ordinarily eight feet high, and those on the second floor are seven and a half feet high.

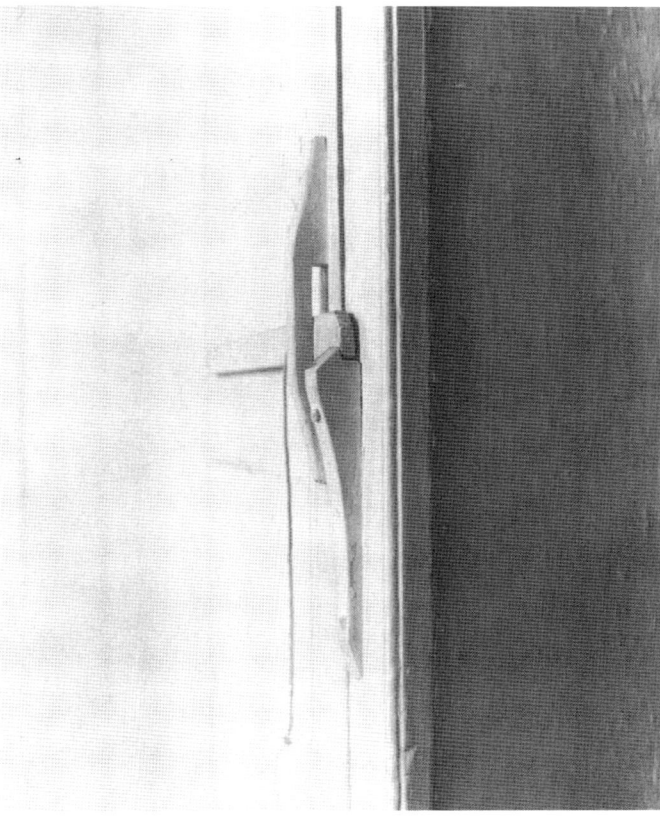

The massive chimney with six flues serving various fireplaces diminishes in size at it comes into the garret. A feature of the garret is the steep ladder stair leading to a skylight in the roof which gives access to the "walk." Here, as in most Nantucket garrets, there is a finished room.

The wooden latch on the batten door to the garret is an extremely graceful one. Its designer has turned a simple utilitarian object into a thing of beauty.

The Maria Mitchell House   101

THE ISAIAH FOLGER HOUSE

In the simple gray-shingled house at 26 Milk
Street, lived Isaiah Folger, fifth son of Walter
Folger, Jr., maker of the famous Folger clock.
In his schooner "Exact," Isaiah took a small
group of settlers from Portland, Oregon, into
Puget Sound in 1851 and landed them at Alki
Point to found the settlement which was to be-
come the city of Seattle, an undertaking des-
cribed by Edna Ferber in her novel, *Great Son*.

102

The house is a typical Nantucket Quaker house of the last quarter of the eighteenth century. Two large closets were removed early in the present century to enlarge an entry *(facing page)* which originally was little more than a passage lighted by a glass "lights" over the front entrance. The front stair has a closed stringer, turned newel post, and square balusters. The furnishings of the entry represent many countries: the hanging lantern comes from Spain, the large chest in the foreground from Sweden, and the smaller chest from Germany. The brass vase is Russian, the red box Chinese, and the Queen Anne fiddle-back chair, made in the mid-1700's, is American in origin.

Although not an authentic restoration, the former kitchen in the Isaiah Folger House does show the construction of a Nantucket fireplace.

The bricks in the upper right-hand corner are new, but the wooden lintel over the fireplace opening is original and was put there to make possible the nailing of paneling. The cooking oven (never called a Dutch oven) at the left has a long, narrow flue directly over the opening, which was necessary since a fire was built in the oven itself to heat the bricks. When these were sufficiently hot, the coals were transferred to the niche below the oven. The sheathing on the wall at the left of the fireplace covers a former closet doorway which has been shifted around the corner. Under this room lies a circular, eight-foot, brick cellar reached by steps from the rear entry at the left.

The painting of the Port of Genoa which hangs over the lamp is by Verney and was brought to Nantucket from Charleston. A Russian tray hangs over the fireplace.

The Isaiah Folger House   103

In the south wall of the former kitchen, a large window has replaced a smaller one in order to take advantage of the sunshine. A tavern table stands before it on the left. The "country" desk is in the Hepplewhite style, and the wall sconces are French tole. A fan-back Windsor is used as a desk chair.

A forerunner of the modern iron circular staircase is this typical back stairway which leads from the back entry to the second floor. This was a development of the winding front stair in the earliest Nantucket houses. The narrow treads and the steepness testify to the adventurous spirit of the Nantucketer; the stair is exceedingly treacherous, and a careless descent can give one the effect of a "Nantucket sleighride." Under these stairs is the ladder stair to the cellar. The electrical outlet in the thin plank partition shows the difficulty of concealing the modernization of an old house.

At the left, a detail of the stair construction, seen from below.

The Isaiah Folger House   105

At the top of the steep ladder stair to the circular cellar, a small batten door opens to reveal a low, tiny closet between the backs of the fireplaces in the large chimney. Such a closet was very likely used for the storage and drying of fruit and vegetables or for the storage of wood to feed six hungry fireplaces, not, as is sometimes romantically supposed, for a retreat from hostile Indians. Nantucket Indians were on the whole quite agreeable. During the Revolutionary War and the War of 1812, the island had far more to fear from the raids of the British and the indifference of the mainland to her exposed position.

The second-floor back bedchamber on the southwest side is accessible from both the front and back stairs. The fireplace wall, after it had been stripped of many layers of wallpaper, revealed a plaster wall with lavender feather graining signed by Sally Starbuck. Unfortunately — or fortunately, depending on one's taste — the wall was in too bad condition to restore.

Above the fireplace is a lithograph of Boston, published in 1848, about the time that Captain Folger was exploring the West Coast in his small schooner. The small chest with curved top, a Nantucket piece, is painted a gray-blue. In the pewter collection on the hanging shelf above it, is a porringer made by William Calder who worked in Providence, Rhode Island, in the early ninteenth century.

The book shelves are a modern addition.

The Isaiah Folger House   107

The upstairs front room in the northeast corner of the house was used as a bedchamber, unless, as often happened when men were away on whaling voyages for three or four years, families doubled up, in which case this room might have become the parlor for the second family.

The fireplace wall is paneled in typical Nan-tucket fashion. The modern tendency to scrape these walls to the natural wood, while effective, is not authentic, for the woodwork in the houses of this period was always painted. The original color used in this room was a light apple green. The ship model was made in Brittany in the nineteenth century and is supposedly the replica of a slave ship.

THE SHUBAEL ALLEN HOUSE

The house at 18 Milk Street, on the southwest corner of the intersection of Milk and New Mill streets, was built late in the eighteenth century and was at one time the home of Captain Allen, who mastered a "Nantucket coaster." Although window sash of six over six panes have replaced the original twelve-over-twelve type, the façade still has projected plank window frames. In plan the house is a duplicate of the Isaiah Folger House at 26 Milk Street. Pos-

sibly they were constructed by the same builder.

In the parlor *(right),* over the eighteenth-century slant-top desk, hangs a water color of the Wright-Chambliss House on Main Street, painted by Edgar W. Jenney. Two decanters and a covered jar of Bohemian glass are used as decoration on the desk. An ornamented black lacquer sewing box of Chinese origin is displayed between the two front windows. Late Sheraton painted chairs stand at the right.

109

The typical paneled wall of Nantucket houses is an unobtrusive background for the more ornate furniture of the Empire and Victorian periods. A tea tray is set with Wedgwood porcelain decorated in France.

The paneling on the fireplace wall in the room which was formerly the kitchen is not the original design. The chimney, however, still contains the cooking oven. The shelf with bulbous brackets had, for some inexplicable reason, great popularity during the late nineteenth century. Originally this wall looked much like that pictured on page 114, but in spite of other changes, the hearth still has the original square bricks.

110   *The Shubael Allen House*

3 PLEASANT STREET

In the houses on Pleasant Street one may trace the development of Nantucket architecture. Representing the typical Nantucket house of the late eighteenth century is the house at 3 Pleasant Street at the head of Summer Street.

Its entrance is a recent restoration, but the projected plank window frames and small-paned sash are original. The "wart" on the south side was made into a two-story ell in the mid-1860's.

111

It is evident from many details that the builder of this house took pride in his craft. The bolection molding on the paneled fireplace wall in the parlor has crossetted corners. Much of the attractiveness found in this type of Nantucket house stems from the emphasis placed on certain elements in the general design, in particular the restriction of paneling to the principal rooms and the simpler treatment of door and window casings in rooms for informal use.

Such distinctions reveal the eighteenth-century sense of fitness for each room in the house, too often lacking in modern houses of this size.

Over the nineteenth-century schoolmaster's desk in the front parlor, hangs an oil painting of a whaling scene found in New Bedford by a former owner of the house. New Bedford, too, was a whaling port and a great rival of Nantucket.

The entry has been enlarged by the removal of the two closets always associated with this plan. The stair, with a heavy, turned pine newel, closed stringer, and turned balusters is typical of the period.

It is unusual to find a paneled fireplace wall in the room behind the parlor, for this room was generally used as a first-floor bedchamber and was therefore simply decorated. The design of the paneling, however, is characteristic of the period of the house, and its presence here is probably an exception to the rule. The well-turned Windsor armchair was made in the latter half of the eighteenth century, but it has suffered the fate of many of these fine examples in having the lower ends of its legs removed and rockers added.

The original treatment of the fireplace wall still remains in the room that was formerly the kitchen and is now used as a dining room. If an authentic restoration had been desired, the fireplace wall in the room pictured on page 103 should have resembled this one.

When not in use, the cooking oven at the left of the fireplace was concealed behind a door. In this instance the door is paneled, but in the room on page 103 a batten type of door was used for it, which was found stored in the attic.

12 WESTMINSTER STREET

The dining room in the old house at 12 Westminster Street contains a fireplace with curved sides. Other examples of this construction exist on Nantucket, but not in great number. The fireplace opening is framed with an iron edge around the inside of the plaster-cement face. In section, this edge is a half-inch square.

The unusual baby's chair with legs flared to prevent it from tipping is in the Chippendale style.

In many Nantucket houses the kitchen was moved to a new ell added to the rear of the structure. If the addition was not made too late in the nineteenth century, it usually had a fireplace with an opening of modest size, built at the end farthest from the original house.

For many years this kitchen fireplace was closed and an iron stove was used for cooking. A modern stove, which requires no chimney flue, has enabled the present owners to reopen the fireplace. An effective sheathed wall has been made from old floor boards taken from the garret and given a natural pine finish. The resulting kitchen is a successful blend of modern appliances and an old background.

115

41 UNION STREET

The paneled fireplace wall in the dining room of the house at 41 Union Street, while extremely effective, is not strictly an authentic restoration. It was made from old floor boards taken from the garret. Dutch tiles compose the fireplace facing instead of the typical painted cement-plaster. Many people find the severity of the Nantucket interior uncompromising, and here we have an example of how well that interior can adapt itself to off-island ideas.

The house, which was built late in the eighteenth century, has the typical plan of a Nantucket house of this period. In the front parlor, simple but good antiques have been used. The restrained lines of a Sheraton sofa make it compatible with older pieces in the room.

116

5 NEW MILL STREET

In the house at 5 New Mill Street are found all the components of the typical Nantucket house. Placed close to the sidewalk, its façade shows weathered gray shingles and projecting plank window frames. The small-paned sash have no weights but are propped open with flat notched sticks. Conservative decoration is evident in the molded caps over the transomed front door and the windows. The house was built in the late eighteenth century and in plan and character is similar to the Maria Mitchell House at 1 Vestal Street.

A ceramic cat from Japan stands guard in the entry. Here, as in many other houses of this period, the entry closet has been removed, providing a well-lighted niche for a Hepplewhite card table and a Windsor armchair. A second newel post, in this instance, has been added.

117

The fireman plays an important role in Nantucket's history. Fire-fighting equipment at the time of the Great Fire in 1846 was, for the most part, owned and maintained by volunteer companies which competed with each other to be the first at the scene of a fire. The first company to arrive had the privilege of playing the hose directly on the fire, and because of this custom the Great Fire was able to gain much headway. Company No. 6 and Company No. 8 arrived at the fire practically at the same moment, and an argument ensued over which should have the position of honor at the fire. The argument was just long enough to allow the flames to spread beyond the Geary store where they had started. This papier-mâché figure represents a fireman of that period from Company No. 8.

On the Hepplewhite cardtable in the entry stand a whale-oil lamp and two unusual French figurines with monkeys' heads on human bodies. Over them hangs a relief model of a full-rigged ship. The wall clock is a reproduction made by Lincoln Ceely, one of the last of Nantucket's fine craftsmen.

Written in pencil on the bottom of one of the figurines is the following couplet: "Monkey saw a baboon sister, Smacked his lips and then he kissed her."

A view of the opposite end of the entry shows the spotted cat in profile. On the drop-leaf table stands "The Handsome Fireman." The door directly ahead opens into what was once the old kitchen, and the one at the right leads to the cellar stair. In this type of house paneled doors are usually hung on butt hinges, while batten doors are hung on HH, HL, or strap hinges.

7 NEW MILL STREET

When the kitchen of a Nantucket house was moved to a new ell built onto the rear, the cooking oven in the old kitchen, being no longer needed, was removed and the space converted into a storeroom for firewood. In some instances, the new ell was only one story high and contained the kitchen and a woodshed. If more bedchambers were needed, a second story would be added to the ell.

The house at 7 New Mill Street was built in the nineteenth century, after cut nails came into use. In plan it is similar to the Maria Mitchell House. Mantels of a uniform design have been used in the parlor (shown here), the room behind the parlor, and two bedchambers on the second floor.

120

26 LIBERTY STREET

This early nineteenth-century house was once the home of Captain Benjamin Worth but saw little of its owner, who made thirty-four voyages, touching the coasts of all continents, in the space of forty-one years. In the latter part of the nineteenth century the house was owned by Captain William Tice, who was in command of the whaleships "Harvest" and "Tyleston."

Furnishings in the house show a collector's taste. While every piece of furniture in the parlor is worthy of attention, the curly-maple desk on frame, made in the middle 1700's, is the most impressive. The low, separate frame has cabriole legs with Dutch feet.

121

Examples from a large collection of fine clocks are found in every room. The banjo clock hanging over the beaded mirror board in the second-floor chamber was made by Lemuel Curtis of Concord, Massachusetts. The lower painted panel depicts the naval engagement between the United States sloop "Hornet" and H. M. S. "Peacock" in the War of 1812.

The treatment of the fireplace wall (above) in the parlor is more ornate than is usually found in a Nantucket house of this period, for here are found fluted pilasters over a bolection molding with crossetted corners.

Standing against the paneling is a tall or grandfather clock made by Aaron Willard, who worked in Roxbury, Massachusetts, in the late eighteenth century.

Another clock of finest quality (left) is the mahogany, inlaid shelf clock with a kidney-shaped dial in the back parlor on the first floor. It was made by Elnathan Taber of Roxbury, Massachusetts, at the end of the eighteenth century and is similar to the one in the M. & M. Karolik Collection at the Museum of Fine Arts in Boston.

The small Chippendale straight-front chest of drawers has bracket feet, and a carved sunburst embellishes the center top drawer. This chest is one of the many pieces in the superb collection of fine curly-maple furniture in the house.

The wide floor boards have been painted in a checkered design, faintly visible in the photograph. This design was sometimes used in place of the painted spattered floor. An early eighteenth-century banister-back armchair stands in the foreground.

Much of the collection of curly maple furniture is concentrated in the dining room. A matched set of six three-slat chairs is used with a Hepplewhite sideboard and a free-standing cabinet, all in that wood.

The rare lighthouse clock on the sideboard was invented and made by Simon Willard early in the nineteenth century. It is an eight-day clock and has a little ship rocking back and forth on the top. A collection of old bottles in soft shades of rose, green and amber is displayed in the bay window, which is a modern addition.

The room behind the parlor, reached by a passway, is used as a sitting room. A country Chippendale chair stands at the left of the fireplace with its early nineteenth-century mantel.

It is somewhat startling to come upon a Queen Anne bonnet-top highboy of such high quality in a secondary bedchamber of a Nantucket house, but the house accepts it with a simple dignity.

Perhaps the most distinguished piece of furniture in the house is the fine mahogany block-front Goddard desk placed in the back sitting room. The Hepplewhite mahogany mirror is a fitting companion piece.

26 Liberty Street   125

In the second-floor front chamber, a Hepplewhite shield-back sidechair of exceptional design shows to advantage against simple Nantucket paneling. The mantel, holding pewter and another shelf clock from the extensive collection, is a later addition.

THE BUNKER-MIXTER-DELL HOUSE

On Academy Hill, overlooking Nantucket Sound, stands the Bunker-Mixter-Dell House, built at the beginning of the nineteenth century and first occupied by Reuben R. Bunker, a whaling captain. The house, while more spacious than most Nantucket houses, retains the typical plan with the rooms clustered around a central chimney serving six fireplaces.

On the exterior, the corners of the house have been embellished with wooden quoins, and the entrance with its simple fanlight over the door has been emphasized by a classical front porch in the Federal style. The front of the building is clapboarded and its sides and back are shingled. Topped by a "walk" and provided with twelve-over-twelve-pane windows irregularly placed in the façade, the house, surrounded by a capped picket fence is a fine example of a seaport dwelling.

In the front hall it is evident that the narrow entry of the Nantucket type of house has been widened to include a window. The paneled dado is unusual in that the dado cap does not stop at the intersection of the corners of the hall and at door frames, but continues down the side to the floor.

127

The newel post in the front hall is reeded on only two sides and the reeding is carried down the stair riser to the floor.

The grandfather clock at the left of the door into the dining room was made by Joseph Fix, who worked in Reading, Pennsylvania, between 1820 and 1840.

A pair of terrestrial and celestial globes flanks the fireplace in the dining room. In the older type of Nantucket dwelling, this room would have been the kitchen, but the paneled fireplace wall and dado here indicate a more formal use. At the time this house was built, the kitchen was usually consigned to an ell in the rear.

The parlor fireplace wall has applied crosset-ted moldings. Cranes are found in practically every Nantucket fireplace; this one was prob-ably intended to hold a tea kettle.

A closet at the right of the parlor fireplace has been fitted with drawers and shelves. One of the latter pulls out, making available a coun-ter for preparing afternoon tea.

Exposed corner-post construction was still used when this house was built, but a casing conceals the rough timber. An added refine-ment is a beaded edge on the casing. A finely carved Empire sofa shares honors with a Chip-pendale armchair. Shown here is an effective way of displaying a ship model by hanging it on the wall.

The Bunker-Mixter-Dell House   129

Behind the parlor is a first-floor guest bedchamber which, with its three large windows and occupying the southeast corner of the house, is bright with sunshine most of the day.

Unlike other rooms in the house, its sheathing and dado do not have raised paneling. The fireplace with curved sides has been built out beyond the face of the wall, and the ashes or sand upon which its fire is laid are confined by a curved piece of metal on the hearth. The wide floor boards are painted and spattered.

A Sheraton fire-screen desk stands at the right of the fireplace; bow Windsors with bamboo-turned legs stand at the foot of the beds.

Two identical Chippendale side chairs with delicately pierced splats and slip seats are placed against the stair railing in the upper hall. The seats are covered with needlepoint worked by the present owner.

Two closets were removed to enlarge the hall which is furnished with a number of noteworthy antiques, including two desks. The one on the left, with a graceful French foot, dates from about 1800.

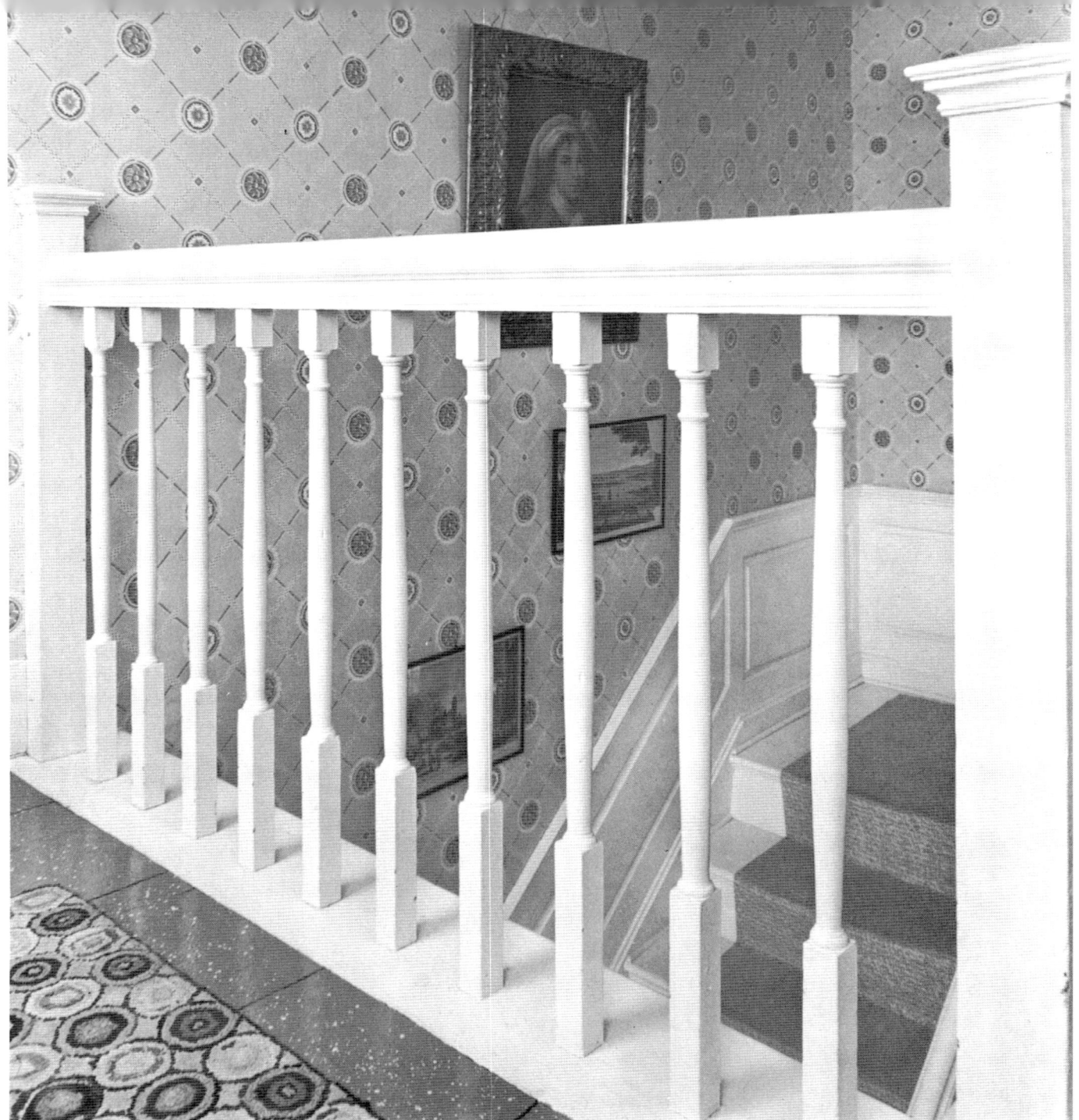

Above, the railing around the stair well in the upper hall.

From the front chamber *(facing page)* over the parlor, one can see the waters of Nantucket Sound. The room is furnished with a bed in the Sheraton style, its posts decorated with reeded tops and unadorned urns. A Queen Anne high-boy holds an early nineteenth-century bandbox covered with scenic wallpaper entitled "Fire Engine B." The mirror over the simple Chippendale chest of drawers is early Empire. Hooked rugs, although mid-nineteenth-century in date, are effective on a painted and spattered floor.

The fireplace opening in this room has been reduced in size. A molded mantel, one of two in the house, has been used around the opening.

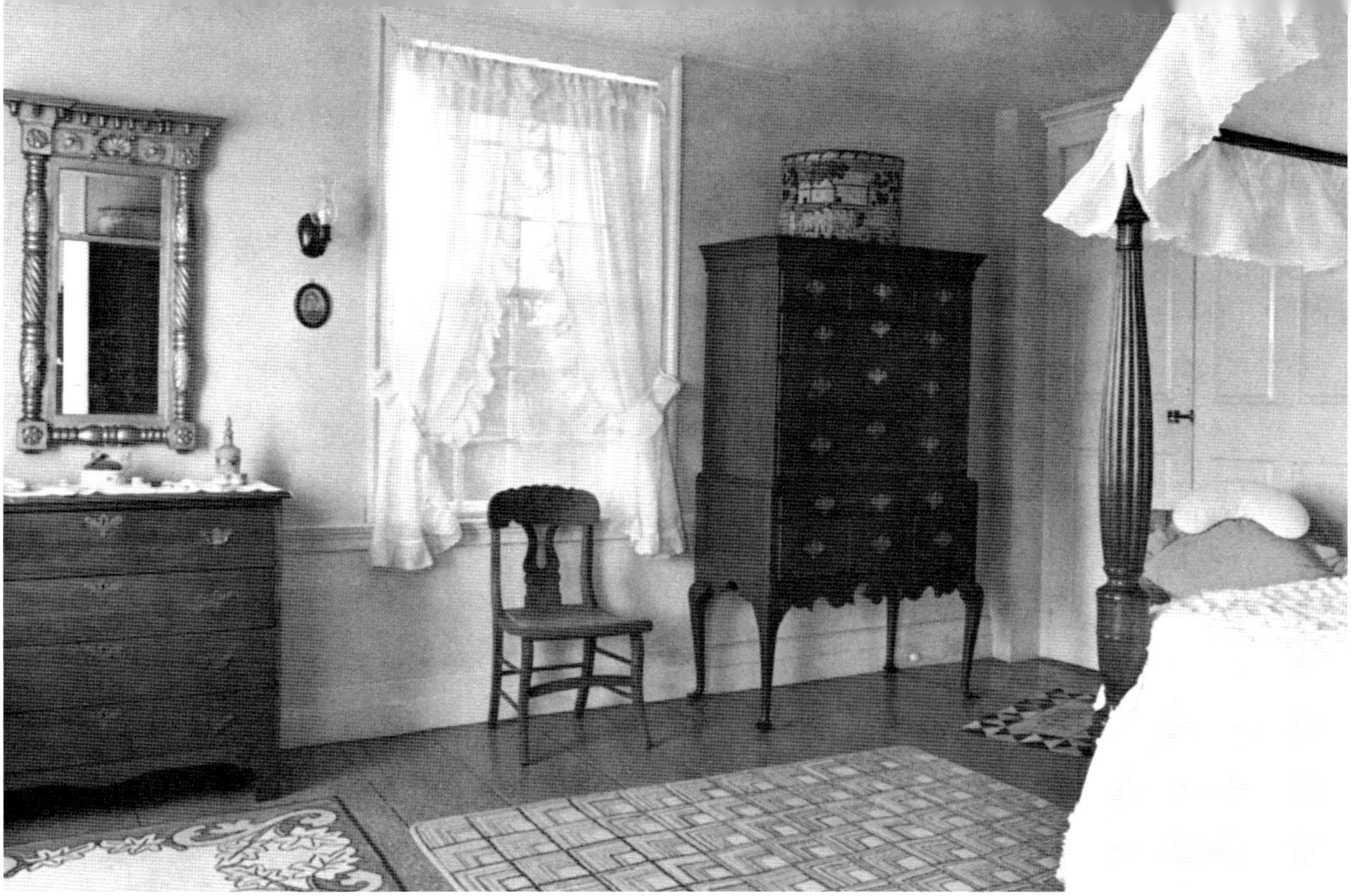

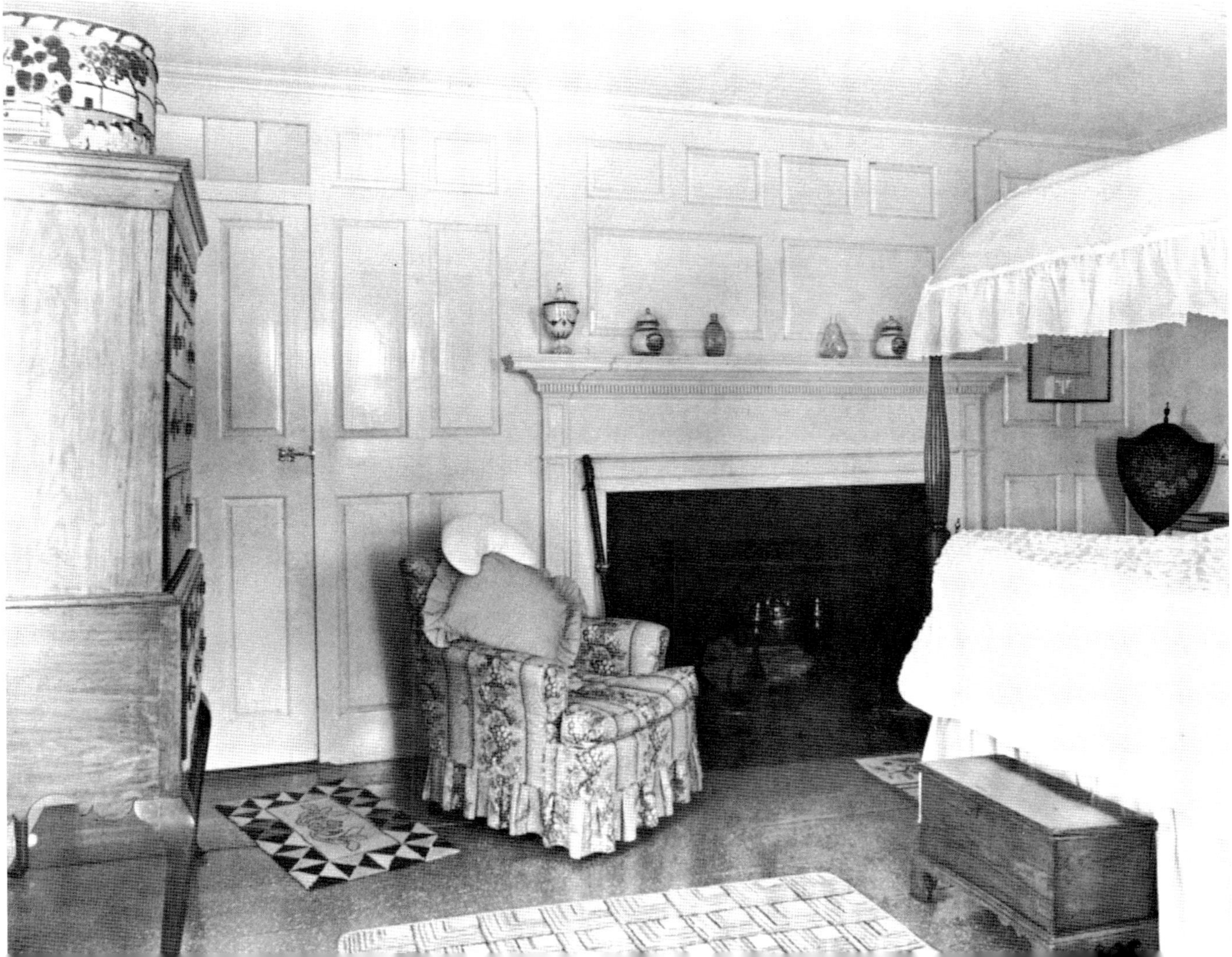

33 MILK STREET

The house on the northeast corner at the intersection of Milk Street and Quaker Lane (formerly Saratoga Street) was built in 1820 by George Coffin and illustrates how accepted forms persisted on the island into the nineteenth century. Although it is still a typical Nantucket house, changes in the basic design indicate new influences at work. The windows all have the same number of panes, unlike older houses which have narrower windows in minor rooms. The off-center arrangement remains, although the entrance has become more ornate, with tapering pilasters supporting a simple entablature.

A comparatively spacious hall *(facing page),* seen through the parlor door, has replaced the long narrow entry of the earlier plan, and the two closets (one opening from the entry, the other opening from the kitchen) have completely disappeared. The additional space makes possible a gracious furniture arrangement. The grandfather clock was made in London by George Prior in 1755. Over the Chippendale chair hangs a little portrait of a child, probably painted by Sally Gardner, who specialized in oils and miniatures of children in the early nineteenth century.

The front parlor woodwork is similar to that in the hall. A plaster dado with a simple beaded base and a wide, molded and beaded dado cap is used on all four walls. The transition from the plaster wall to the ceiling is eased by a simple cornice. The doors in this house lack raised panels, an indication of nineteenth-century workmanship. Over the eighteenth-century slat-back chair hangs an oil painting of Captain Owen Spooner, the whaler who discovered a navigational aid known as "sunset longitude." The astral lamp on the table in the foreground is sometimes called a "dangler" lamp because of the dangling glass prisms.

The front parlor retains an atmosphere that has practically disappeared in our fast-moving age as it sits poised for any social emergency. A mantel in early Greek Revival style has been substituted for the typical paneling around the fireplace opening. Exposed corner-post construction has disappeared.

On the wall at the left is an oil portrait of William Bunker Gardner, master of the "Sarah Parker" and the "Columbus" and ancestor of the present owner of the house.

The sewing cabinet was made by sailors on the "Sarah Parker" and presented to their captain's daughter, Charlotte Coffin Gardner.

136   *33 Milk Street*

The tidy bedchamber behind the parlor on the first floor is furnished with early nineteenth-century furniture.

The woodwork in the bedchamber *(below)* over the parlor is similar to that in the parlor, except that a paneled dado has been added. The table at the left was made by sailors on board the "Sarah Parker."

The back stair to the second floor is in the ell built at the same time as the main section of the house. The bottom step with curved bracket end is not enclosed behind the batten door; this is a typical treatment of this element.

The kitchen has purposely not been modernized and remains as it was in the nineteenth century. The painting of the walls to simulate grained wood is a restoration.

The
Post-Revolutionary
Period

The Post-Revolutionary Period

BEING a small island has disadvantages as well as advantages. Nantucket lost 134 vessels and 1600 men to the British during the trying years between 1775 and 1783, but with peace restored, the ocean once more became the island's highway to the world and her ships began to make longer whaling voyages. In 1791 the "Beaver," the first Nantucket whaling vessel to round hazardous Cape Horn, sailed into the Pacific and was among the first ships to open up those new whaling grounds and begin the great whaling era that was to make the island well-known to the world. And the wealth brought to Nantucket by an increasing number of successful whaling voyages enabled the inhabitants to build larger houses.

Psychological and practical needs for keeping up with the changing times eventually helped outside influences to overcome some of Quaker conventionalism, and toward the end of the eighteenth century the Federal style of architecture, already in full swing on the mainland, began to find expression on the island. Houses with a central hall separating the rooms on either side began to be built, even though older plans continued to be used well into the nineteenth century.

Dwellings constructed on the new central-hall plan still kept many building methods long established on the island. They were set high on brick foundations in which windows lighted a full basement. An entrance placed in the center of the façade with two windows on either side was given more importance by using side lights in addition to the lights over the door and by adding flat, tapering pilasters carrying a simple entablature. Projected plank window frames continued to be used, but the panes of glass in the sash became larger in size and fewer in number. Each sash contained six 9″ x 12″ panes, making a six-over-six-paned window.

The post-and-girt frame construction continued to be used, but the timbers were lightened by the use of studs between the posts. Several brick dwellings were constructed at this time, but wood construction predominated until the second quarter of the nineteenth century. The gambrel roof made an appearance but never became popular on the island.

The central stair hall grew to be spacious according to Nantucket standards, and the stair railing was often embellished with a volute. Ceilings were made higher and the construction was hidden between walls and floor whenever it was possible to do so. Fireplace openings in all principal rooms were of similar size and were framed by wooden mantels with shelves. Two or four chimneys served the fireplaces instead of the single central chimney found in older plans. Wood paneling continued to be used on the fireplace wall, but as the nineteenth century progressed, a sunken panel was used in preference to the raised panel.

The Federal style, however, never attained on Nantucket the elegant delicacy it achieved on the mainland, due in part to the continuing Quaker influence and in part to the lack of great wealth on the island. The patriotic motifs characteristic of Federal style, eagles, stars and the like, are also conspicuously absent in island architecture; religious disapproval and anger at the Federal government's disregard for the island's welfare in time of war were sufficient to suppress any widespread use of such symbols. Elegance had to wait for the decline of the Quaker faith and for the fortunes made at the peak of the whaling industry in the second quarter of the nineteenth century, which coincided with the Greek Revival period on the mainland.

3 ACADEMY LANE

Academy Hill, once known as Beacon Hill, has its share of distinctive Nantucket houses. Among these is the one at 3 Academy Lane built in the last quarter of the eighteenth century by one of the descendants of an original proprietor, Richard Gardner. In plan the house is similar to the earlier two-story lean-to, but here the rear rises to two full stories, and the treatment of the interior shows late eighteenth-century influence. A central chimney contains the six fireplaces that originally heated the house.

The front entry has been enlarged by the addition of a vestibule at the front of the house which, while probably built at the same time as the house, is not a typical Nantucket feature.

143

The enlarged entry *(facing page)* has the usual winding stair. The four corners of the square newel posts have beaded edges, and vertical boards with beaded joints sheathe the stair well as far as the second floor. The Hepplewhite sideboard, seen through the doorway to the dining room, has over it an early nineteenth-century mirror designed to be used over a mantel. In it is reflected a hanging shelf on which is displayed old china pitchers and teapots.

In the dining room late Empire chairs are used at a Hepplewhite table. Nantucket houses were probably never furnished in one consistent style, but each generation contributed its taste to the family house, with the result that these interiors have a liveable, rather than museumlike appearance.

The fireplace is a simple one, consisting merely of a flat bolection molding applied to a flat board frame. The mantel with its bulbous supports is a later addition.

At the right, a view of the front entry from the parlor.

The dentils on the cornice of the fireplace wall of the right front parlor are a special point of interest. Although a restrained detail of ornamentation, their appearance seems most unusual in a Nantucket house. A similar cornice and paneled wall appear in the corresponding bedchamber on the second floor.

An inlaid Hepplewhite card table and a Hepplewhite tambour desk are important pieces in this room. The chair at the right of the fireplace is "country" Chippendale, and the armchair at the left is early nineteenth century.

A glimpse of the right front parlor from the front entry. The door in the distance opens into a back entry which contains a stair to the second floor and which may be entered from a side entrance. Such a side entrance is rarely found in Nantucket.

THE 1800 HOUSE — The Nantucket Historical Society

One of the few houses open to the public in the summer months is The 1800 House at 4 Mill Street, owned by the Nantucket Historical Society. It was built in 1801 by Richard L. Coleman, housewright, who later transferred it to Jeremiah Lawrence, High Sheriff for the County.

The house is an example of the continuation of the older lean-to house plan, with a two-story rear portion making possible well-lighted rooms at the back of the second floor. Oak sills, laid on a fieldstone foundation, carry two oak beams extending from the front to the rear

on either side of a chimney eight and a half feet square. The first floor joists are crudely hewn from tree trunks.

The newel post of the front stair is similar to that in the Captain Richard Gardner House on West Chester Street which is a much older house (see page 30). This particular turning is a popular one and found in work of the late eighteenth century. It is therefore possible that the stair in the earlier house on West Chester Street is a replacement, for the stair in houses of its period ordinarily had no turned newel post and balusters or molded handrail.

In the east parlor at the left of the small entry, the fireplace wall is simply paneled in the Nantucket fashion. The door at the left gives access to the "keeping room" at the rear of the house. Aaron Willard of Roxbury, Massachusetts, made the mahogany grandfather clock.

The parlor has been furnished from the collection donated to the Historical Society. The two-section desk and chest of drawers was made of camphorwood in China for Captain Oliver C. Spencer and was used in his cabin aboard the steamer "Lamont," owned by the Shanghai Steam Navigation Company, before it was brought to the island in 1866. On the desk are a pair of Victorian shell vases with glass shade covers.

The portrait is of the Reverend George Bradburn, an early abolitionist, pastor of the First Universalist Church in Nantucket sometime between 1827 and 1834, and representative to the General Court, 1839 through 1841. The portrait was painted in 1849 by Hathaway and was rescued from the Atheneum during the Great Fire.

148   *The 1800 House*

The "keeping room" is an early New England expression for the common dwelling room where the family also cooked and ate. The keeping room in this house is furnished with pieces ranging in date from 1750 to 1850. The chair at the left of the desk is Chippendale, and a nineteenth-century Hitchcock chair stands at the right.

The treatment of the walls in the keeping room varies. The long fireplace wall is paneled, while the east wall is sheathed with vertical boards decorated with a narrow bead at the joints. The south and west walls are plastered.

The narrow door at the right opens into a closet, space once occupied by a cooking oven. The bricks in the hearth are set in sand, an old island practice. The child's high chair at the table, the doll and the small chair in which it is sitting are all nineteenth-century pieces.

The present kitchen lies in an old one-and-a-half-story building added to the rear of the house after Jeremiah Lawrence bought the property.

The 1800 House   151

5 ORANGE STREET

One of the few examples of the gambrel roof, never popular on the island, is to be found at 5 Orange Street. The house also has the distinction of being one of Nantucket's earliest brick house; its date of construction is said to have been 1774.

The plan of the dwelling is the central hall type with two rooms on either side, each with a fireplace on the outside wall. Originally only the two ends of the building were brick; the wooden front and back were replaced with brick after the Great Fire of 1846. The house was on the fringe of the fire and actually helped to stop its devastating progress, but the front was badly damaged.

A large collection of ivory-headed canes occupies a prominent space near the front entrance.

152

It can be seen from the Greek Revival forms of the door casings and fireplace mantels that much of the interior woodwork was replaced after the Great Fire.

The early corner cabinet, while not of the same period as the house, seems at home with its elegant neighbors, a Sheraton sofa and a Queen Anne side chair with Spanish feet. The successful mingling of furniture and art objects of various periods in this house testifies to the sound taste of the owner in these matters.

The opening between the rooms, enlarged in the nineteenth century, makes a double parlor furnished with many fine antiques, notable among which is the maple secretary-cabinet with its broken-arch top and Dutch bandy legs. An early eighteenth-century corner chair with a rush seat is used as a desk chair.

The back south parlor (below) has been made into a comfortable library. The silhouettes and miniatures at the right are only a few examples from a large collection scattered throughout the house.

The dining room contains a set of Sheraton-style chairs with shuttled reeds and carved ovals. The paneling is probably original, but the china cabinets are later additions.

The late eighteenth-century serving table or small sideboard in the Hepplewhite style has doors and drawers inlaid with quarter-circular panel outlines. The silver coffee urn is a noteworthy piece.

THE HINCHMAN HOUSE — *Maria Mitchell Association*

The Hinchman House at 7 Milk Street on the south corner of Vestal Street, now owned by the Nantucket Maria Mitchell Association, was built in the early part of the nineteenth century and was originally called the Thomas Coffin House.

In plan the house is of the two story, central-hall type with two rooms on either side of the hall. Two chimneys provide a fireplace in each of the eight rooms in the main part of the house. It is built on a high brick foundation and has in the basement a summer kitchen with fireplace and beehive cooking oven.

The entrance, with tapering pilasters and a cornice, a local interpretation of the Federal style, has a distinct Nantucket flavor in its effective combination of true functionalism and restrained decoration.

157

The side lights and transoms around the front door provide the hall with ample light. A simple stair climbs to the second floor. The whalebone button at the top of the newel post in the center of the volute is supposed to show that there is no mortgage on the house.

The building and the natural history collection which it houses have an important position in Nantucket's summer life. Here those interested in the island's flora and fauna may identify specimens gathered after a day's roaming on the moors and beaches. The organization also has classes and field trips for children.

Mantels are used against paneled walls in the two front parlors; this one is in the parlor on the right. The paneling is not of the raised type, characteristic of the eighteenth century; instead, a sunken panel has been used with a narrow molding. The reeded molding on the mantel is typical of late eighteenth- and early nineteenth-century work, but the woodwork of this period on Nantucket never reached the sophistication found in the work of Samuel McIntire of Salem.

The Hinchman House   159

The house is an excellent example of the type built on Nantucket in the early nineteenth century. Here are some of the elements found in a typical Nantucket interior: simple and restrained woodwork, lights over an interior door, and a chest of drawers built into the wall.

The simplicity of the Hinchman House makes a fitting background for the Nantucket wildflowers which are displayed in season in all the rooms on the first floor. Shown in the dining room are various arrangements which should encourage the use of wildflowers in the décor of old rooms.

160 *The Hinchman House*

The
Siasconset Cottage

The Siasconset Cottage

WHILE the indigenous Nantucket house was developing in "The Town" around Great Harbor, another type of dwelling was unconsciously being evolved on a bluff seven miles away at the southeastern extremity of the island. Here, two and a half miles apart, at two settlements called Sachacha and Siasconset, fishermen were building temporary shelters for protection during the spring and fall cod-fishing seasons. These settlements, overlooking a broad expanse of the Atlantic, were locally known as fishing "stands" or "stages." The structures which composed them were crude one-room affairs with dirt floors. Cooking was done in the open air or on open porches. Eventually the settlement at Sachacha was abandoned, and many of its shanties were moved to Siasconset, or 'Sconset as it is known to islanders. As time went on islanders found the area a delightful place for outings, and fishermen's families began to spend more and more time there during the summer months.

Since the one-room shanties were inadequate to shelter comfortably an entire family, the fishermen began to add to them in all directions, using odds and ends as materials. Old doors and windows of varying sizes, which were no longer needed in town, were brought here and installed in the additions. Parts of ships wrecked on the treacherous shoals around the island found their way into the structures. Floors were laid; chimneys and fireplaces were added. Porches were enclosed, but the term "porch" continued to be used to designate a kitchen.

Such additions were called "warts" and were generally too small to provide room for more than a narrow bed or cot. Often the "wart" acquired a second story, providing a small, low bedchamber for the small fry, who reached their room by climbing a cleat ladder nailed to the wall.

By the early nineteenth century the settlement at 'Sconset had reached the status of a village and was becoming a popular summer resort for Nantucketers who lived in the town. By this time, too, a casual and somehow homogeneous seaside architecture had developed, the specimens of which defy definite dating. The little houses, looking very much like dwellings for Lilliputians, are still being added to, and the early fishermen would never recognize their one-room shanties in the comparatively luxurious homes of this fashionable summer resort.

THE GARDNER HOUSE

The George C. Gardner house on Broadway in 'Sconset has fortunately escaped alteration and looks today much as it did in the early nineteenth century. It was built by Prince Gardner, but as is the case with most of these little fishing shacks that "just grew" into houses for the summer folk, the actual date of building has never been recorded. This house is known to have been in existence before 1814. The main section contains an entry and a parlor with an ample fireplace. The addition with a shed roof, called a porch, houses a large kitchen, and the "warts" on the south side provide the bedchambers.

The parlor with its spacious fireplace has two views, one of the street and one of the ocean. Beyond the horizon lies no land until one reaches Spain. A roaring fire is not only welcomed but needed when the fog that waits offshore moves inland.

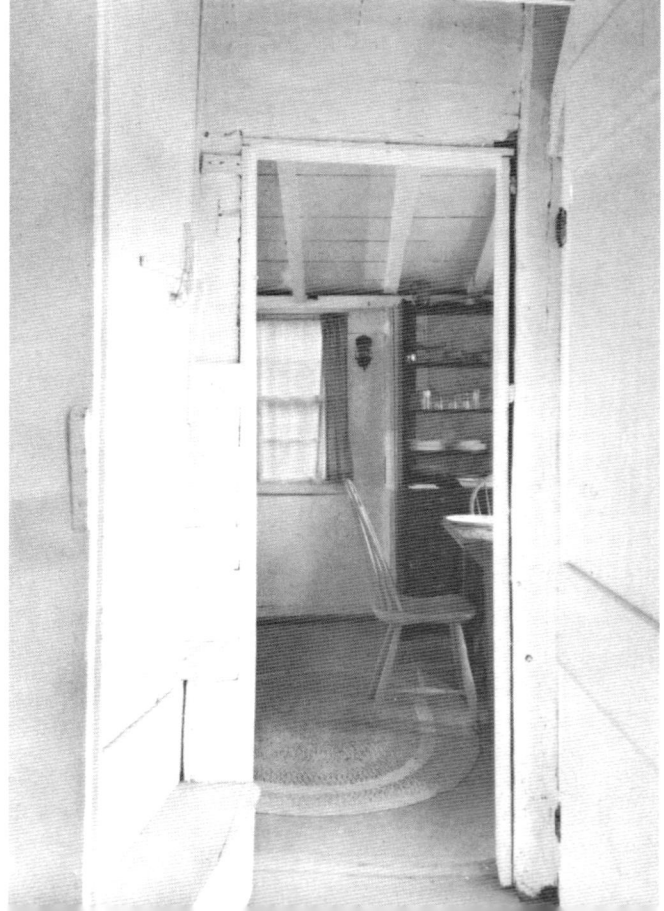

The kitchen in the north ell is equipped with a coal stove. Bow-back Windsor chairs are used at the table in the dining area. From the window one has a sweeping view of the ocean.

From the little entry on the east or ocean side, one can reach the kitchen and parlor, and by opening the batten door at the left, can climb up a steep stairway to the garret.

NONANTUM

Further up Broadway and on the same side of the street, is a house, named Nonantum, that grew and grew and grew. Originally a small one-story dwelling built by Barzillai Folger early in the nineteenth century, during the ensuing years it not only grew "warts" but also a second story. The parlor is suitably furnished with antiques. An early map of Nantucket Island hangs over a chest of drawers with bracket feet and Hepplewhite brasses.

The fireplace mantel is a delightfully naive interpretation of a late eighteenth-century design, probably made by a country carpenter depending on simple tools and his memory of a design he had seen.

The small study on the east side of the house contains a fireplace and a stair to the second floor. This is the original section of the house. The fireplace wall is decorated with objects connected with the sea: harpoon irons and maps. On the mantel is a collection of scrimshaw made from whale teeth.

'Sconset houses were made from scrap lumber picked up along the beaches after a shipwreck and from buildings in Nantucket Town that had outlived their usefulness. In Nonantum the newel post looks very much like the end of a church pew. The handrail does not go through the post, although it gives that appearance.

When Nonantum was first built, it had no formal dining room such as the one seen here. The ship model hull under the window is used as a flower box, and the ship's lantern over it adds another nautical touch.

WILLOW HARP

The house to the north of Nonantum, called Willow Harp, was built by Benjamin Bunker early in the nineteenth century. Long known as Columbia Cottage, the house was given its more romantic name fairly recently. Willow Harp is supposedly derived from a remark sailors would exchange as their ship passed close to land: "Matey, can you hear the Willow Harp? Land is near," referring to the wind whistling in the willow trees ashore.

The house was once tiny and had many windows of all shapes and sizes, as well as seven outside doors. Numerous "warts" have been added, and today the house contains a living room, dining room, kitchen, five bedrooms and two and a half bathrooms. There is no hint of rigorous life in a fishing shack to be seen in the present furnishings, for the house has all the comforts of a New York apartment.

169

A door in the dining room leads to a small terrace on the north side of the house. Here a flower border blooms throughout the summer and far into the mild Nantucket autumn. At dinnertime light is supplied by a row of candles on the brick chimney shelf.

The little bedchamber reached by a ladder in the parlor is characteristic of a 'Sconset house. This room was usually given to the children, who went to bed by climbing on cleats nailed to the wall beneath the tiny opening.

THE CORNERS

The old cottage between Center and Shell streets north of the pump has not been spoiled by recent additions. It has its share of "warts," but these add to rather than detract from its charm. It was owned early in the nineteenth century by Shubael Barnard and for many years was called Meerheim. The exterior does not prepare one for the relatively spacious interior which contains an entry, parlor, large kitchen, three bedchambers and a bath.

The living room at the left of the tiny entry contains a large fireplace. The door at the left opens into a closet. Simple antique furnishings have been wisely chosen for this cottage and make themselves at home without difficulty.

The old batten door in the entry opens to a
steep ladder stair to the garret. The only handrail provided is a hanging knotted rope.

The chair at the left of the fireplace is a Windsor from the early nineteenth century. The tiny entry can be glimpsed through the door.

The fishermen who came out to 'Sconset during the codfishing season would never recognize their crude fishing shacks, now grown into comfortable dwellings furnished with arrow-back Windsors, hooked rugs, and pictures.

The largest bedchamber boasts a Sheraton
canopy bed, a fireplace, and four windows,
two of which, looking out on Shell Street, have
been placed close to the ceiling.

The Greek Revival Period

The Greek Revival
Period

FROM 1812 to 1815, the years of the war between the new country and England momentarily hampered Nantucket's growing prosperity. The War of 1812 was fought mainly on the sea. Although Nantucket tried to remain neutral, she again lost vessels and men and her livelihood was reduced to a low ebb. Fortunately the war was short-lived, and when peace was declared in 1815, the island's whaling vessels were again free to hunt down the valuable whale on the high seas unmolested.

By the mid-1830's shipowners and captains of this whaling fleet had become comparatively wealthy and well-traveled men, and their contact with all parts of the world had developed in them an appreciation of the amenities of life. Most of these men remained members of the Society of Friends, but the purity and strength of the early years of the movement had gone. In the 1820's, for the first time, controversy in the Society of Friends had resulted in a division in its ranks. Another controversy followed, coming to a climax in 1838, irreparably weakening Quaker domination on the island.

Changes, too, were taking place on the mainland. The primitive colonizing era, as far as the Eastern seaboard was concerned, had definitely come to an end. America as a country was coming into its own. There was now time to look around at literature and the arts. Sparked by the Greek struggle for independence, a new style in architecture and decoration, called Greek Revival, was sweeping the large seaports and smaller inland towns and villages of the growing country.

The spread of this vigorous style coincided with Nantucket's most prosperous period, the decades between 1820 and 1850, and much of its atmosphere of a successful and wealthy American seaport is due to the examples of Greek Revival architecture found in some form on almost every street in the town. Nantucket's houses in this style are generally conservative in manner, since old building traditions remained strong in the face of changing styles, and the Quaker faith, although waning as a formal religion, still reinforced a certain degree of restraint already ingrained in the character of the islanders. The new fashion was limited at first to minor details. While exteriors continue to show the influence of Georgian and Federal styles found on the mainland, porches and interior decoration begin to reveal elements of Greek Revival treatment. Many of the elements of the new style are concentrated in wooden and marble fireplace mantels and on the interior trim of doors and windows.

Brick was used as well as wood, and for the first time on the island, houses were built that were impressive enough to be called mansions. Plans provided for double parlors connected by large openings with sliding doors, so that they could be thrown together for entertaining large groups. Many of the older, eighteenth-century houses show the effects of this era of prosperity by having acquired in the 1830's and 1840's heavy entrances in the Greek Revival style.

By 1846, the year of Nantucket's Great Fire, the island's population had reached 10,000 inhabitants and its prosperity had reached a peak. Isaiah Folger's copy of *Hayward's Massachusetts Gazetteer* describes in detail the basis and extent of this thriving era.

> The whale fishery commenced here in 1690; and this place is, perhaps, more celebrated than any other, for the enterprise and success of its people, in that species of nautical adventure. Indeed, Nantucket is the mother of that great branch of wealth in America, if not in the world. In the year ending April 1, 1844, Nantucket employed seventy-eight vessels in that fishery, the tonnage of which was twenty-six thousand six hundred and eighty-four tons; one million eighty-six thousand four hundred and eighty-eight gallons of sperm and whale oil were imported, the value of which was eight hundred and forty-six thousand dollars. The number of hands employed was about two thousand. The capital invested was two million seven hundred and thirty thousand dollars; this includes the ships and outfits only; yet many of the manufactories of the place are appendages of the whale fishery; altogether employing a capital of five millions of dollars.

> There are manufactures on the island, of vessels, whale boats, bar iron, tin-ware, boots, shoes, oil casks, and candle boxes. The whole amount of the manufactures of oil and candles, in 1844, was one million three hundred and

seventy-five thousand seven hundred and forty-five dollars. Total tonnage of the district of Nantucket in 1844, thirty-thousand six hundred and ninety-seven tons.

After the ruinous fire of July 13, 1846, in which one third, the center, of the town was destroyed, the new style began to be used in its most vigorous form, producing some fine examples of Greek Revival style in domestic and public buildings.

Nantucket would probably have recovered from the disastrous effects of the fire, but the discovery of methods to refine crude oil for illumination in 1855 was a death blow to the whaling industry. From then on Nantucket's importance as a commercial port rapidly diminished. The California Gold Rush of 1848 claimed many of its sons. During the second half of the nineteenth century, Nantucket became a drowsy town with a dwindling population, for in order to live many of its inhabitants were forced to move to the mainland. As a result, from the Civil War to the twentieth century, there was little building in the town, and it was, therefore, providentially spared most of the extravagances of the Victorian era. Today Nantucket Town and 'Sconset, again bustling with social and commercial activity, retain along their quiet streets and lanes, lined with simple, dignified buildings, the atmosphere of a less complex age.

16 VESTAL STREET

The one-and-a-half story lean-to at 16 Vestal Street is in Greek Revival style but has, nevertheless, a definite Nantucket flavor. The entrance, once at the front of the house, is now in the gabled end. The house is built around a chimney serving three fireplaces, two on the first floor and one on the second. No exposed corner posts are visible in the interior; therefore, in spite of its early lean-to design, the house was probably built in the nineteenth century.

In the front parlor a Greek Revival mantel, displaying four pieces of Bohemian glass, frames the fireplace opening which the grouping of furniture makes the focal point of the room. The severe Empire soft has a fan motif carved on its skirt board.

The absence of window curtains gives importance to the woodwork in the front parlor and makes it a frame for the pictures of the changing seasons outside. A Windsor armchair with bamboo turnings is silhouetted against a Chippendale secretary with ogee bracket feet, made about 1770. The venerable ladder-back rocker is an island piece, while the spice box on the table at the left is an item from the Maria Mitchell homestead.

Presiding over the dining room is a mid-eighteenth-century grandfather clock. The rush-bottom dining room chairs are Empire, and the china closet is a strictly utilitarian one.

The front parlor has been decorated with restraint by a descendant of the Mitchells who was brought up in a Quaker household.

The carving on the newel post in the hall is similar to that often found on the legs of Empire tables. The doors in the house are of the six-panel type often called Christian doors. The one visible through the hall doorway has "lights" in the top panels and a "kitty-cat door," with its own knob and button, in the lower left panel.

A bedchamber under the sloping roof at the back, in many ways one of the most interesting rooms in the house, is called the Rafter Room. Here it is possible to see the construction of an old house. Wide horizontal sheathing has been nailed to posts spaced over two feet from center to center. Notable among the room's furnishings are a Sheraton four-post bed, with two of the posts richly carved with acanthus leaves, drapery, and tassels, and a fine upholstered mid-eighteenth-century Queen Anne child's chair from Newport, Rhode Island. The iron monster behind the chair becomes a friendly companion when the cold winds blow across Nantucket in January. The washstand, appropriately equipped, and the gilt mirror above it date from the nineteenth century and came from the Maria Mitchell homestead.

32 MILK STREET

The house on the southeast corner of the intersection of Milk and Mt. Vernon streets was first owned by Captain Calvin Worth, but this whaler got little enjoyment from his property, for he spent but two months ashore between 1841 and 1849 when his whaleship "United States" was lost in the South Pacific. The house was occupied by his two sisters Lydia and Margaret, and was eventually sold to Henry W. Barrally and known for a long time as the Barrally House.

The fireplace mantel in the front parlor is of more delicate design than many found in this type of Greek Revival house. At the right of the much used fireplace stands a fine Chippendale ladder-back chair with fluted legs. The roundabout chair at the left dates from the early eighteenth century.

20 UNION STREET

The large house at 20 Union Street was built in the 1830's. Similar in plan to the Three Bricks on Main Street, the house, of the central-hall type, has four chimneys on the side walls. Close to the style of the Federal period, the exterior does not prepare one for the Greek Revival woodwork found inside. The entrance has none of the solidity usually found in the design of this period. Graceful, tapering pilasters support a simple, light entablature and cornice, and the characteristic transom appears over the door. Inside, exposed corner posts are still visible, although the beams they carry have been concealed between the floors.

In the hall a free-standing post supports the landing above, giving the design a shipboard atmosphere as well as providing a newel post for the railing which is used instead of a solid wall.

The heavy, turned newel post is another note of solidity reminiscent of ship construction. In spite of the Greek Revival woodwork, many older structural methods have been used in the framing.

184

Another nautical note is found in the ship-shape built-in drawers between two bedchambers on the second floor. The wallpaper on the foreground walls is a Chinese tea-box paper. A Sears Roebuck catalogue has been used to make the Oriental-looking doorstop on the floor.

WALLACE HALL — Nantucket Historical Trust

But for the resoluteness of Mrs. Lydia Barrett, there would have been no imposing white mansion at 72 Main Street to photograph for this book. During the Great Fire, Mrs. Barrett, learning that the firefighters intended to blow up her house in order to check the flames licking their way up Main Street, firmly refused to leave. Fortunately, during the delay, the wind changed direction and the flames turned northward.

The house was built in 1820 by John Wendell Barrett and is an example of the Greek Revival style in an early, conservative phase. The front porch with two pairs of columns topped by Ionic capitals is the predominant feature of the façade. The large cupola, a development of the "walk" on the earlier houses, commands a fine view of the harbor and allows one to watch its shipping activity in comfort.

The spacious hall *(facing page)*, running from front to rear through the center of the house, is lighted by sidelights and a transom with leaded panes of glass around the front door. Louvered blinds not only temper the light, but insure privacy.

The stair, delicate in design, has an unusual newel post of brass in the center of the hand-rail volute, a truly nautical touch. The molded door frame with ornamented corners is typical of the Greek Revival period. Beyond lies the west front parlor.

In the west front parlor is a black marble mantel, a fine background for the brass fire frame and fender. An ornate gilt-framed mirror hangs above it. All the windows on the first floor have pedimented cornices.

The mantel in the west rear parlor is of the same design as that in the front parlor but is executed in wood and painted white. The brass fittings are identical for both fireplaces. Large plaster rosettes are used in the centers of the ceilings.

THE HENRY COFFIN HOUSE

The large brick house at 75 Main Street can safely be called one of Nantucket's mansions. It was built in 1833 by Henry Coffin, brother of Charles G. Coffin who built the brick house across the street at 78 Main Street. The brothers were merchants, candle manufacturers and owners of some of Nantucket's best-known whaling ships.

The influence of Greek Revival design is scarcely evident on the exterior, except at the entrance where round pilasters support a simple entablature and frame the recessed door with its sidelights. Because of their stylistic restraint, the brick mansions on the island are often referred to as Georgian in style, but, in fact, the Georgian age as an artistic period had come to an end long before George IV died in 1830.

The four black marble fireplaces on the first floor are identical. An oil portrait of the builder hangs over the one in the east front parlor. His desk at the left was made on the island. The cast-iron fire frame has applied zinc ornamentation.

According to an account book found in the attic, the house cost Henry Coffin $8,200 and the land $3,800. One hundred fifty thousand bricks, brought from the mainland, were required in the construction. The house is still owned by one of his descendants.

Above the Sheraton sideboard in the dining room hangs a portrait of Charles Frederick Coffin, son of Henry, which was painted by J. S. Hathaway, a Nantucketer who had a studio in the Atheneum.

The grandfather clock standing between the windows in the east front parlor originally belonged to Micajah Coffin, in 1734, and has come down in the family to the present owner, his great-grandson. The Windsor chair at the right was made in Nantucket in 1797 by Frederick Slade.

The graceful curve and full sweep of the front stair may be seen in this view from the dining room.

The Henry Coffin House   191

Noteworthy among the furniture in the west back parlor is a Duncan Phyfe trestle-form chess table of early nineteenth-century date, made with swinging shelves to hold candlesticks. An oil portrait of the present owner of the house hangs over the fireplace.

Above the fireplace in the west front parlor is an oil portrait of Levi Starbuck, a brother of Joseph who built the Three Bricks. Levi was in command of the ship "Harlequin" on three successive voyages out of Nantucket in 1799, 1803, and 1808. He made the wing chair at the left in 1797.

Upstairs, at the front of the house, is a smaller bedchamber for a child. Charles Frederick Coffin, the subject of the portrait in the dining room, would feel completely at home in it.

In the second-floor west front chamber is a Sheraton-style bed made in the late eighteenth century. Its carved front posts have a draped urn design with reeding above. Dimly visible through the fish-net canopy hangs another Hathaway portrait, this one of a daughter of Henry Coffin. A fine Hepplewhite tambour desk stands between the front and side windows. The fire screen at the left of the fireplace is Empire.

The Henry Coffin House   193

WEST BRICK

The identical brick mansions at 93, 95 and 97 Main Street are probably the best known houses in Nantucket. Popularly referred to as The Three Bricks, they are designated as East Brick, Middle Brick and West Brick. They were commissioned by Joseph Starbuck for his three sons, William, Matthew, and George, and were constructed in the late 1830's by Christopher Capen, master mason, and James Childs, carpenter. Joseph Starbuck, born in the house at 11 Milk Street, was a butcher early in his career, but through his interests in Nantucket's growing whaling fleet, he became one of the island's most successful whaling merchants. His own house was at 4 New Dollar Lane (formerly Risdale Street) and The Three Bricks were at first kept in his possession until deeded to his sons in 1850.

These photographs of West Brick at 97 Main Street were taken early in the twentieth century when the house was still owned by descendants of the Starbuck family, and they therefore show much of the original furnishings.

The interiors, while similar, are not identical in the three houses; for example, in West Brick all the fireplace mantels are made of wood. The first meeting of the Nantucket Historical Society was held in the west front parlor of West Brick. The décor of this room is characteristic of the early twentieth century, but most of the furniture is contemporary with the house and the Empire style prevails. The fine mid-eighteenth-century Queen Anne upholstered armchair behind the slip-covered Victorian sidechair shows that good old furniture was not discarded to make room for the latest styles.

The east front parlor in West Brick has a mantel identical with those in the other three rooms. Here the décor is more formal. Gilt window cornices were used with draped curtains. The heavily carved circular table is late Empire, and in the corner stands another mid-eighteenth-century Queen Anne wing chair. The gilt mirror, reflecting the fireplace mantel, still remains in the house today.

A heavily carved canopy bed dominates the east front chamber on the second floor of West Brick, a room which gives an excellent impression of how The Three Bricks were originally furnished in late Empire style. Glass "lights" were still used at the time these houses were built, but instead of being set in the walls over the doors, the glass has been placed here in the top panel of the doors.

The wooden fireplace mantels in the second-floor chambers of West Brick are simpler than those on the first floor.

EAST BRICK

East Brick at 93 Main Street was built for William Starbuck, youngest of Joseph's three sons, who lived there until his death in 1873.

The Greek Revival style of the mansion, with its white portico with Ionic columns, was a distinct departure from the traditional style of architecture that prevailed in the Quaker town earlier in the nineteenth century. It reflects the taste of a prosperous merchant.

197

The front and back halls run through the house flanked by two rooms on either side. The double parlor at the right is furnished with a simple elegance appropriate to this style of house. No attempt has been made to limit the furniture to the Empire style. A beige patterned wallpaper has been used in both rooms and the curtains, too, are beige behind gilt cornices.

At the side of a mahogany drum table in the Sheraton style stands a Martha Washington armchair. Over both black marble mantels hang oil portraits of the school of Sir Joshua Reynolds.

The newel post of the stairway is similar to those in other houses built at this time. Simple round balusters accent the flat, pierced-scroll bracket under the treads.

Above, a closer view of the black marble mantels and the portraits in the east double parlor.

In the west front parlor, now the library, is a mantel of like design. The mantel decorations are large figurines of Edward VII as the Prince of Wales on the left and Louis Napoleon on the right, both Staffordshire. Ten smaller figurines, representing Napoleon and his nine generals, are each marked on the bottom with an "N" and crown, the identification mark of Capo-di-Monte porcelain.

The original west double parlor has been divided, with bookshelves added in the library on either side of a doorway leading to the dining room.

Wooden mantels frame the fireplace openings on the second floor. The bedchamber over the front west parlor contains an early nineteenth-century bed with unusually heavy posts supporting a canopy. The decorative flower border used as a cornice and window trim gives the room a Victorian flavor which is enhanced by furniture in the same style.

The bedchamber over the back east parlor has a wooden mantel with Ionic pilasters. The four-post bed with painted decoration is Victorian. At the right of the fireplace is an armless rocking chair, one of two pieces of Starbuck furniture remaining in the house.

East Brick 201

14 ORANGE STREET

Contrasting with its more typically Nantucket neighbors, one of the more unrestrained examples of the Classical Revival style on the island is the house at 14 Orange Street. The plan placing the main façade at the side offers a leisurely approach to the front entrance. This entrance possibly once had a longer porch with four Ionic columns instead of the present two and, also, steps facing the street, for two columns are still stored in the attic. The house, built in the 1830's by William H. Andrews, became the home of Captain James Codd whose successful whaling voyages are attested by his purchase of the house. One of Captain Codd's ships was the "Massachusetts."

The double parlor *(facing page)* on the street side of the house has one of the most elaborate plaster cornices on the island. Until recently the painted wall decoration was covered by wallpaper, and eventually it will be restored to its original condition. The furniture in these rooms shows how a variety of styles can be used effectively where purity of style would seem to be indicated. Chairs in French Directoire style mingle harmoniously with the pair of English crystal candelabra and Chinese jar on the mantel shelf, as well as with the Chippendale chair and Pembroke table of an earlier century. The rug is needlepoint.

The mantel, typical of the period, manages in spite of its heaviness to retain an unobtrusive dignity that remains subordinate to the cornice.

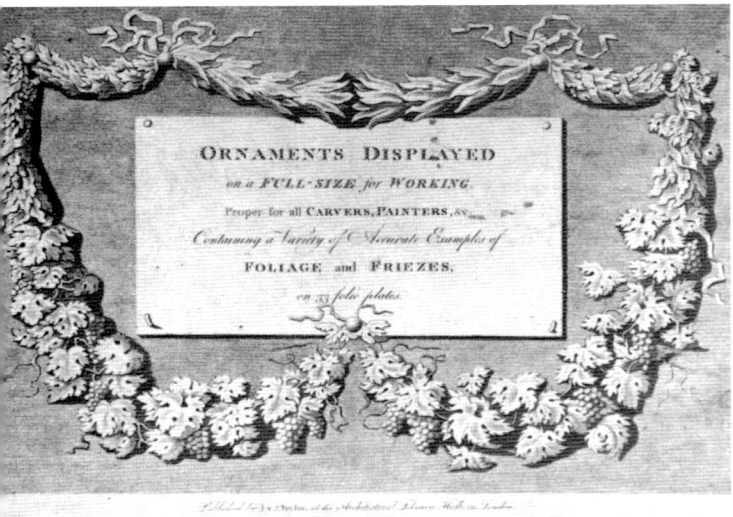

The design of the plaster cornice in the southwest parlor was inspired by the grapevine design used as cover decoration on the English pattern book pictured above. The pattern book, printed in lithograph, was found in the attic of the house.

Two captive lead dolphins (originally used as garden ornaments) disport themselves on either side of the study fireplace. A ship model shares the mantel shelf with a pair of carved stone Chinese seals, used in China to authenticate personal signatures.

The entrance hall, with its stair curving up to the second floor, is lighted not only by lights on either side of the front door, but also by a circular window let into the floor of the garret over which is a skylight in the roof. The stairway in Greek Revival houses on the island was not decorated with the characteristic motifs of that style. The plain, round baluster and simple handrail are closer in style to the Federal period, as is the bracket under the treads. A heavily turned newel post, not pictured, is the only indication of the Greek Revival style.

14 Orange Street   205

THE WRIGHT MANSION

The Wright Mansion at 94 Main Street, also known as the Chambliss House, is one of the group that creates the atmosphere of elegance and wealth on Nantucket's best-known street. The fruit of successful commercial enterprise, these mansions were owned by people closely related, not only by blood but by business interests connected with whaling.

The house, a product of the Classical Revival, was constructed by Frederick Brown Coleman in the mid-1840's when Nantucket was at the peak of success as a whaling port. William Hadwen, who commissioned the building, was a son-in-law of Joseph Starbuck who commissioned the famous "Three Bricks" directly across the street. Hadwen's marriage to Eunice Starbuck, second daughter of Joseph,

was childless, and the couple, becoming fond of a niece, Mary G. Swain, adopted the girl, and it was for her that he built the elaborate house next to his own at 96 Main Street.

Fluted columns with modified Corinthian capitals supporting a wide, ornate entablature and pediment make the façade a graphic proof of the decline of Quaker faith and its restrictions against ostentation. Here we have a design intended to create an impression.

The house is more Roman than Greek in design, and the interior with its applied plaster rosettes and ornaments has many of the elements found in the work of the Adam brothers, although interpreted in a somewhat heavy manner.

A small hall with a simple staircase momentarily dims the impression of grandeur created by the façade; but as one glances up to the second floor, a domed ceiling embellished with plaster rosettes and a niched statue reaffirm the feeling of classical dignity. The dome is supported by a wide entablature and pilasters with Corinthian capitals.

Pilasters form the door and window casings.
Four niches with appropriate classical statues
complete the decoration of an unusual hall
which prepares a visitor for the domed ballroom to come on the second floor.

208   *The Wright Mansion*

The "dome room" is perhaps the most unusual room on the island. Now used as a bedchamber, it originally served as a ballroom. The room was constructed with a spring floor. Beneath the flooring, which did not quite reach the walls, rungs resembling barrel staves were placed which enabled the floor to give when crowded with dancers, thus protecting the plastered ceiling below from direct vibration.

There was once a pulley-operated window in the apex of each dome in the house through which the sky could be seen. These windows were at one time replaced by tiny pieces of colored glass.

The Wright Mansion   209

The double parlor at the right of the hallway on the first floor is less spectacular than the dome room above and is furnished in a friendly Nantucket manner, with disregard for the grandeur that was Rome. Two Windsor armchairs, setting a note of informality, occupy the opening between the front and back rooms.

Both rooms contain furniture from various periods. Hooked rugs have been used on a painted and spattered floor. The bookcases are modern. A Hepplewhite filigree mirror is an important piece in the room. The agate game in the foreground is a form of solitaire and is said to have been invented by a prisoner in the Bastille.

9 PLEASANT STREET

Pleasant Street has its share of houses in the Greek Revival style, of which the house at number 9 is one. It was constructed in the 1830's by John Coleman, brother of Frederick Brown Coleman, and was for many years the home of Benjamin Easton, a well-known Nantucket silversmith. In plan the house is only one room wide with the front entrance, accentuated by a porch with Doric columns, at one side of the façade. In this house, however, an earlier Nantucket influence still prevails, for the gabled end is not at the front as would be expected in this style.

The front hall, with a curving stair to the second floor, is well lighted, not only by a side-light on either side of the door, but also by a window in the side wall.

211

A pair of old English Bristol spill vases with cut-crystal prisms and French tole baskets with pierced rims are used as mantel garniture in the front parlor. The bowl and ewer on the nest of lacquered tables are of rose-medallion Canton ware. The gilt-framed picture done in wool embroidery above is entitled "Shepherdess of the Alps."

The front and back parlors are separated by a large opening with sliding doors, a typical nineteenth-century plan which permitted two main rooms to be opened into one for large entertainments. Such rooms in Greek Revival houses show clearly a change in the scale of living made possible by new whaling fortunes and an increased worldliness stemming from contact with the mainland.

Identical black marble mantels, carved with a shell motif, have been used in the front and back parlors. Their presence in what is essentially a Greek Revival house gives a hint of the Victorian style to come. The rooms are appropriately furnished with Empire and Victorian pieces which give an excellent idea how the rooms might have looked in the mid-1800's.

The white marble mantels in the two main bedchambers on the second floor are more informal, with their carved rose motif, than those in the parlors.

LARGE 6 FLUE BRICK
CHIMNEY USUALLY
PAINTED OR PLASTERED

"WALK" REACHED THROUGH
SKYLIGHT IN ROOF

UPSTAIRS PASSAGE
9/9 WINDOW

PLANK FRAMES
PROJECT FROM
WALL

CLOSET
9/9 WINDOW

PARLOR
BEDCHAMBER
12/12 WINDOW

ENTRY CLOSET
9/9 WINDOW

KITCHEN ELL
USUALLY A LATER
ADDITION

PARLOR
12/12 WINDOW

SHINGLES USUALLY
LEFT TO WEATHER
GREY

HOUSE SET CLOSE
TO SIDEWALK AND
IS ALMOST ENTIRE
WIDTH OF LOT

OFF CENTER DOOR
WITH TRANSOM
TO FRONT ENTRY

CAPPED PICKET
FENCE

WOODEN STEPS
AND PLATFORM

The Typical Nantucket House, Façade (p. 90)

Appendix

Measured Drawings of the Typical Nantucket House

The measured drawings in this section deal only with that house which is a local product of Nantucket. Hundreds of them were built in the late eighteenth century, and all are similar in design and detail. Although the details in the following drawings have been taken from specific houses, they should be considered generally representative of this type of house. It should be noted, however, that two basic plans developed which, while similar, may still be easily differentiated by a comparison of the floor plans on pages 215 and 217.

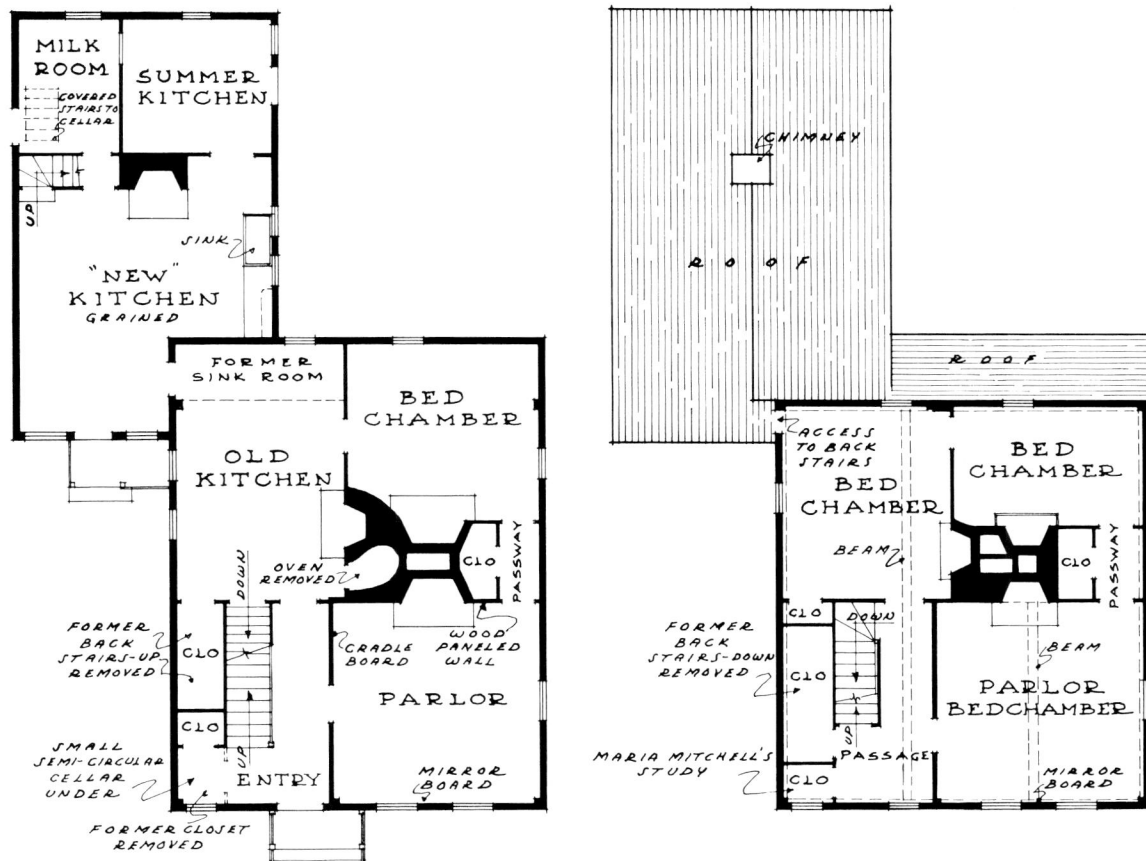

·FIRST·FLOOR·PLAN·   ·SECOND·FLOOR·PLAN·

SCALE

The Typical Nantucket House, Floor Plans (pp. 90-101)
The Maria Mitchell House   215

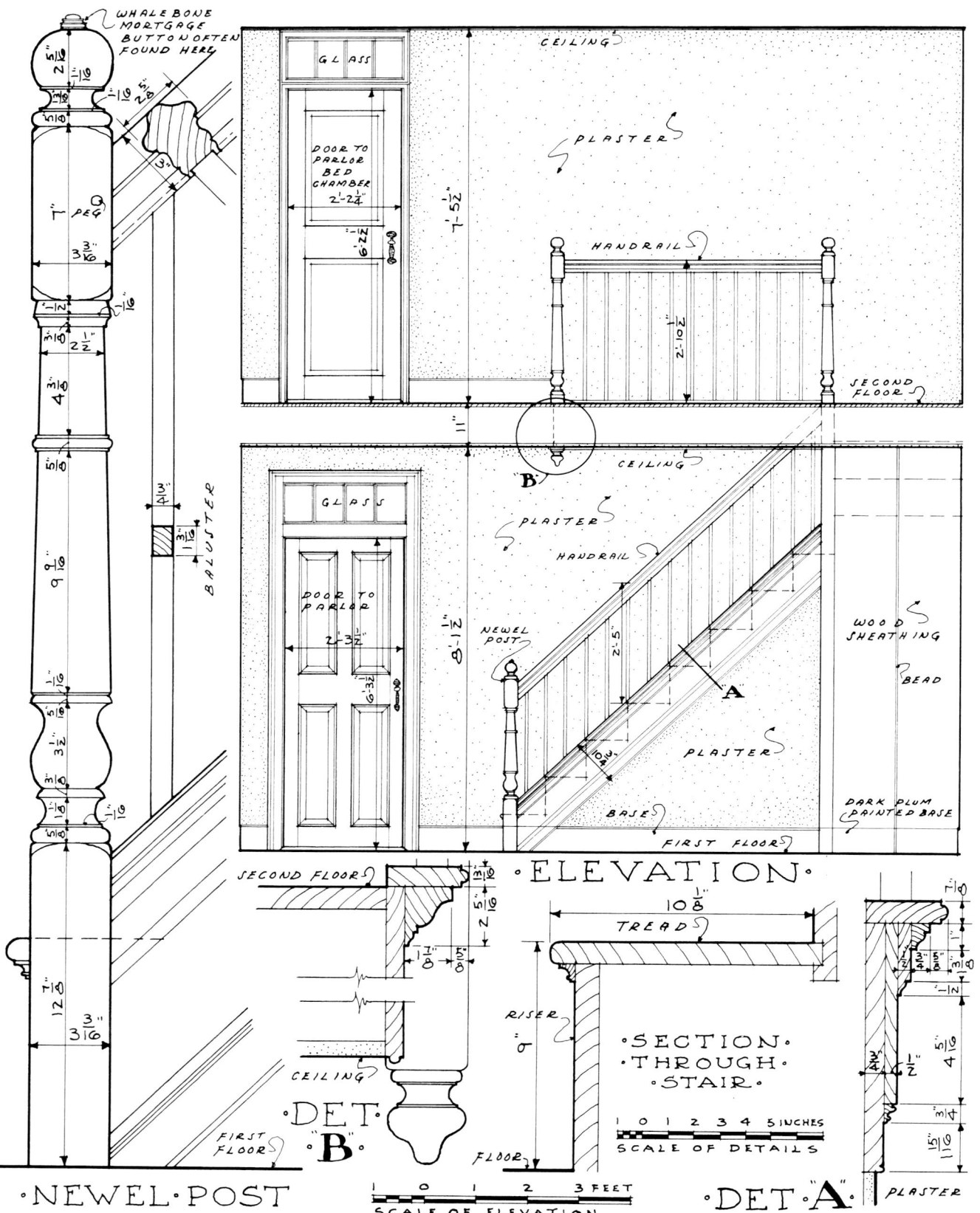

WHALEBONE MORTGAGE BUTTON OFTEN FOUND HERE

GLASS

DOOR TO PARLOR BED CHAMBER
2'-2¼"

CEILING

PLASTER

HANDRAIL

SECOND FLOOR

7'-5½"

2'-10½"

B

CEILING

PLASTER

HANDRAIL

WOOD SHEATHING

BEAD

GLASS

DOOR TO PARLOR
2'-3½"

NEWEL POST

2'-5"

A

PLASTER

8'-1½"

10½"

BASE

DARK PLUM PAINTED BASE

FIRST FLOOR

·ELEVATION·

PEG

BALUSTER

SECOND FLOORS

·DET "B"·

CEILING

FIRST FLOOR

·NEWEL·POST·

12¾"   3³⁄₁₆"

TREAD   10⅛"

RISER
9"

·SECTION·
·THROUGH·
·STAIR·

FLOOR

1 0 1 2 3 FEET
·SCALE OF ELEVATION·

0 1 2 3 4 5 INCHES
·SCALE OF DETAILS·

·DET "A"·

PLASTER

Entry, Stair, and Second-floor Passway (p. 102)

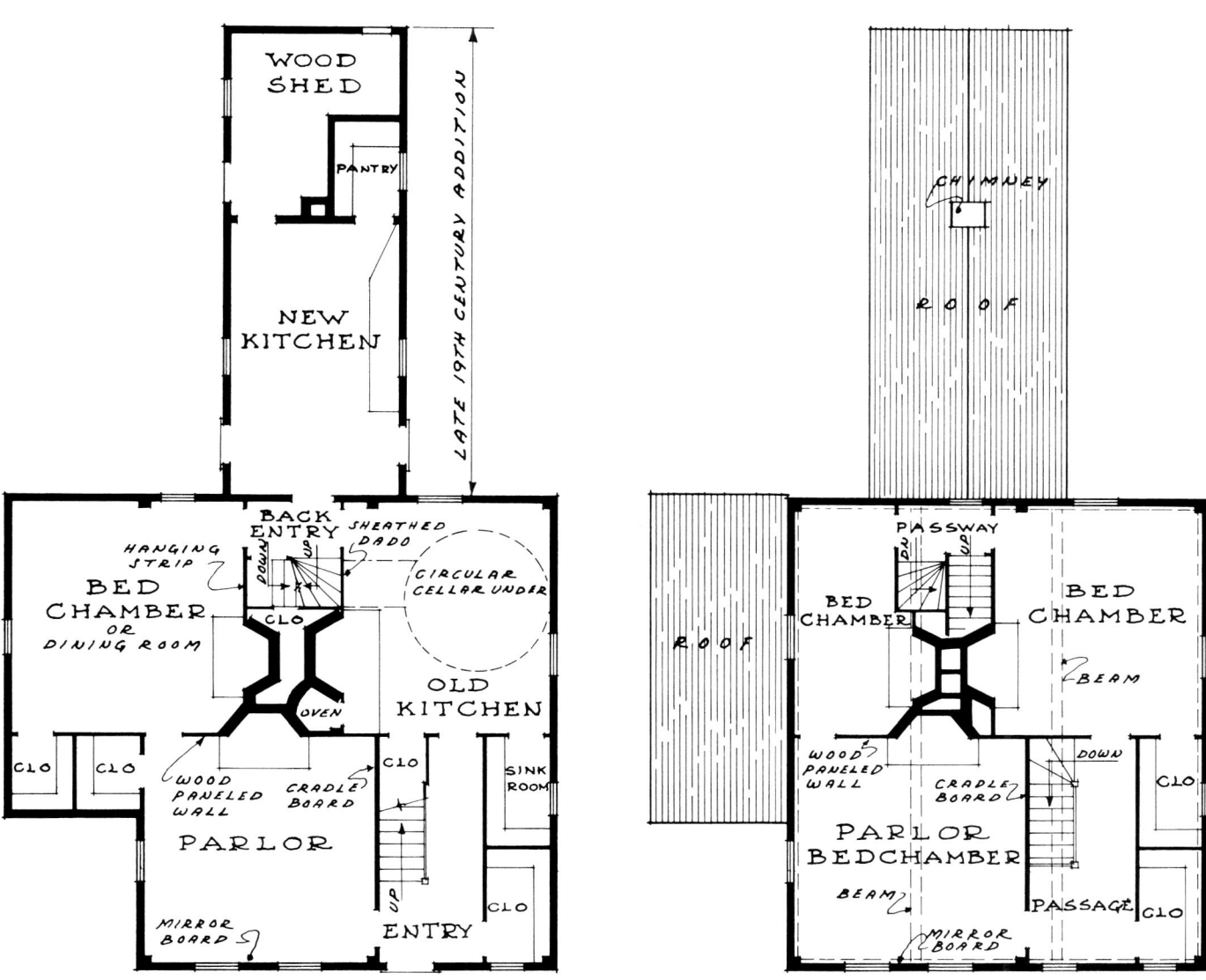

·FIRST·FLOOR·PLAN·   ·SECOND·FLOOR·PLAN·

SCALE

Floor Plans (pp. 102-108)
The Isaiah Folger House   217

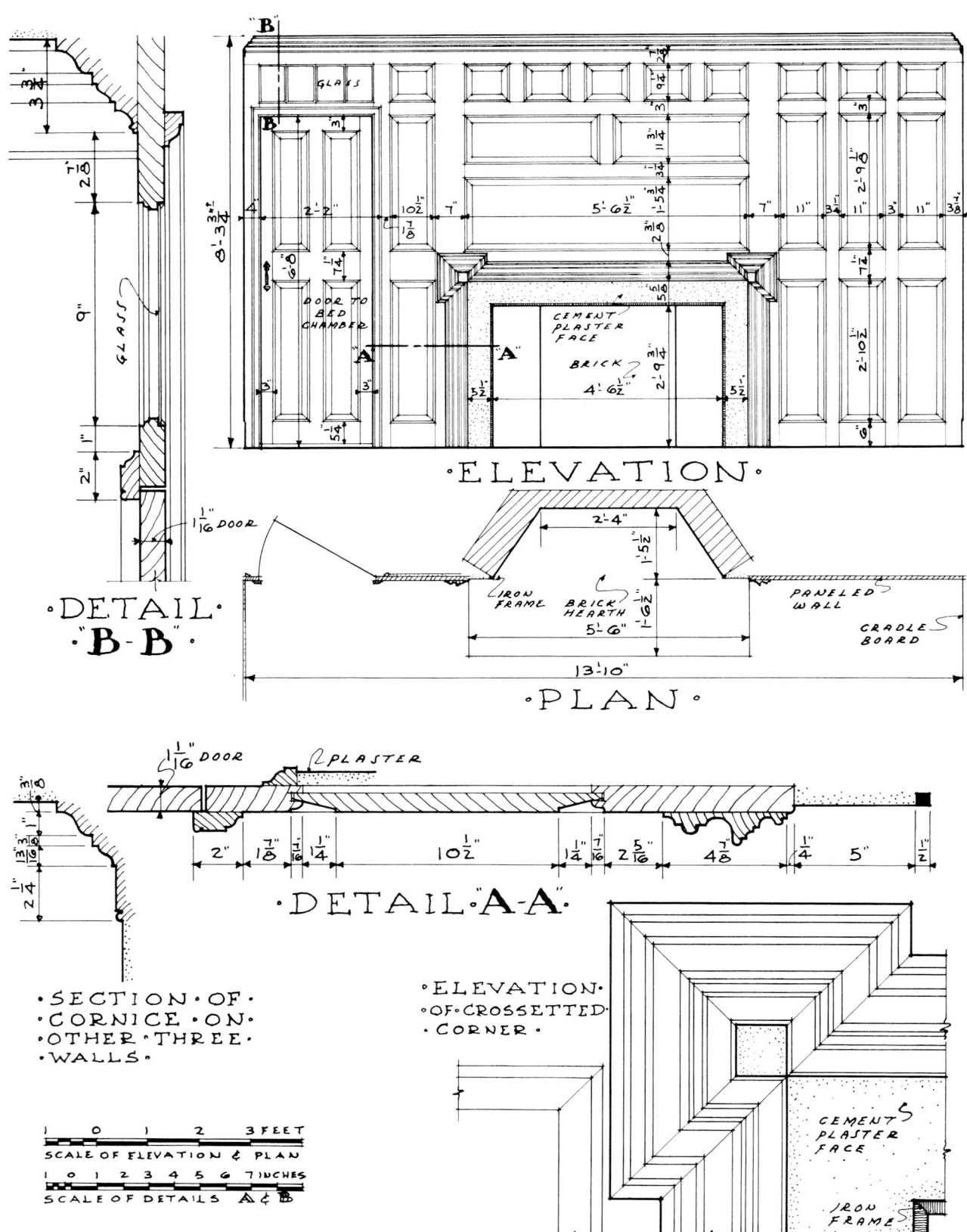

·ELEVATION·

·DETAIL· ·B-B·

·PLAN·

·DETAIL·"A-A"

·SECTION·OF·
·CORNICE·ON·
·OTHER·THREE·
·WALLS·

·ELEVATION·
·OF·CROSSETTED·
·CORNER·

GLASS

DOOR TO
BED
CHAMBER

CEMENT
PLASTER
FACE

BRICK

IRON
FRAME

BRICK
HEARTH

PANELED
WALL

CRADLE
BOARD

1 1/16" DOOR

PLASTER

CEMENT
PLASTER
FACE

IRON
FRAME

SCALE OF ELEVATION & PLAN

SCALE OF DETAILS A & B

Parlor Fireplace Wall (p. 112)

218   *3 Pleasant Street*

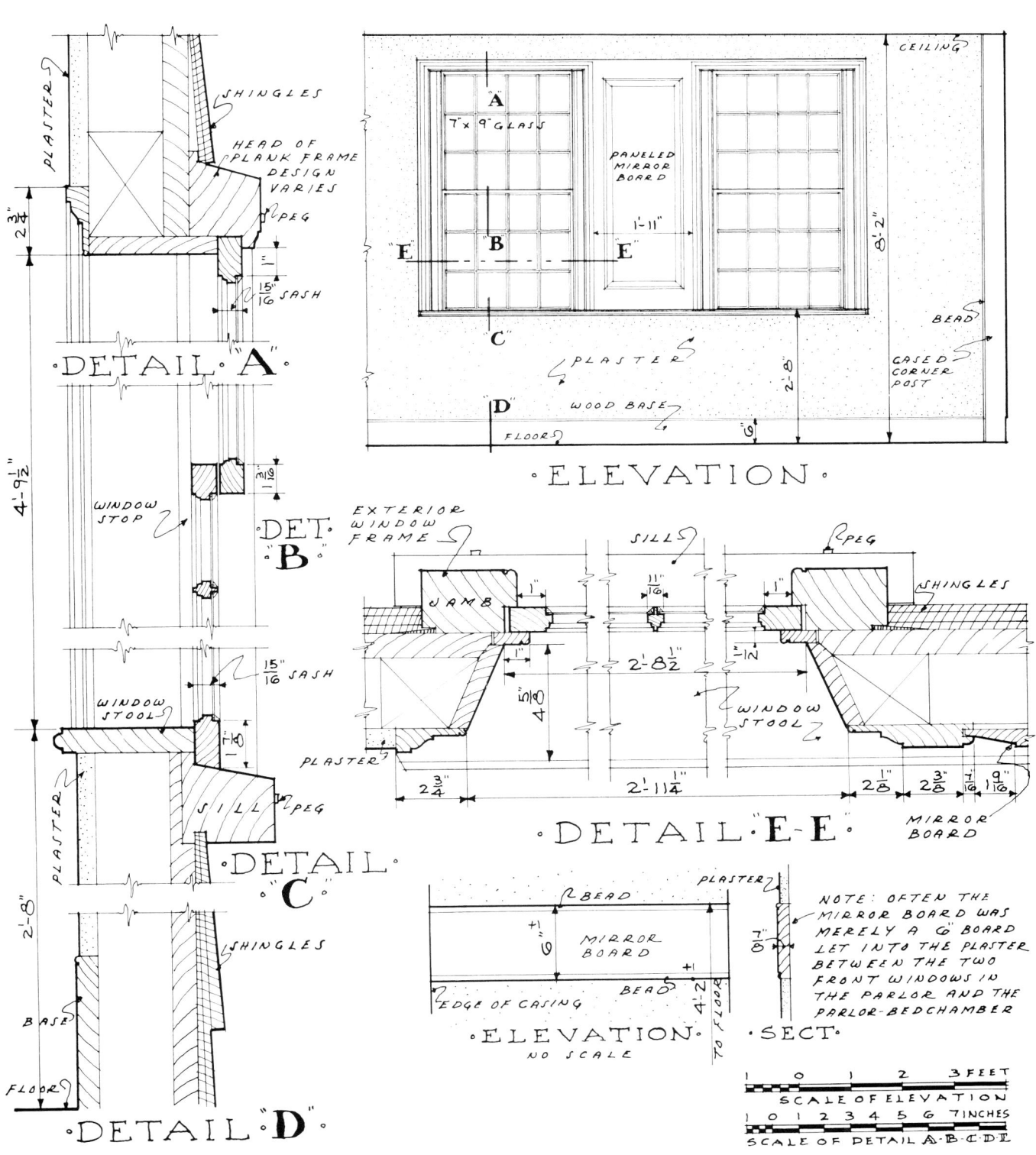

PLASTER

SHINGLES

HEAD OF
PLANK FRAME
DESIGN
VARIES

PEG

2¾"

1"

$\frac{15}{16}$" SASH

· DETAIL · "A" ·

WINDOW
STOP

DET.
"B"

$\frac{3}{10}$"

4'-9½"

$\frac{15}{16}$" SASH

WINDOW
STOOL

PLASTER

SILL

PEG

· DETAIL ·
· "C"

2'-8"

PLASTER

SHINGLES

BASE

FLOOR

· DETAIL · "D" ·

CEILING

A

7"x 9" GLASS

PANELED
MIRROR
BOARD

1'-11"

8'-2"

B

E   E

BEAD

C

CASED
CORNER
POST

2'-8"

PLASTER

D

WOOD BASE

6"

FLOOR

· ELEVATION ·

EXTERIOR
WINDOW
FRAME

SILL

PEG

SHINGLES

JAMB

1"

$\frac{11}{16}$"

1"

$1\frac{1}{2}$"

2'-8½"

5⅕"
4⅕"

WINDOW
STOOL

PLASTER

2¾"

2'-11¼"

2⅛" 2⅜" $\frac{7}{16}$" $\frac{9}{16}$"

MIRROR
BOARD

· DETAIL · E-E ·

BEAD

PLASTER

6"

MIRROR
BOARD

6"

7"

EDGE OF CASING

BEAD

4'-2"

TO FLOOR

· ELEVATION ·
NO SCALE

· SECT ·

NOTE: OFTEN THE
MIRROR BOARD WAS
MERELY A 6" BOARD
LET INTO THE PLASTER
BETWEEN THE TWO
FRONT WINDOWS IN
THE PARLOR AND THE
PARLOR-BEDCHAMBER

1   0   1   2   3 FEET
SCALE OF ELEVATION
1 0 1 2 3 4 5 6 7 INCHES
SCALE OF DETAIL A·B·C·D·E

Parlor Mirror-board Wall
5 New Mill Street   219

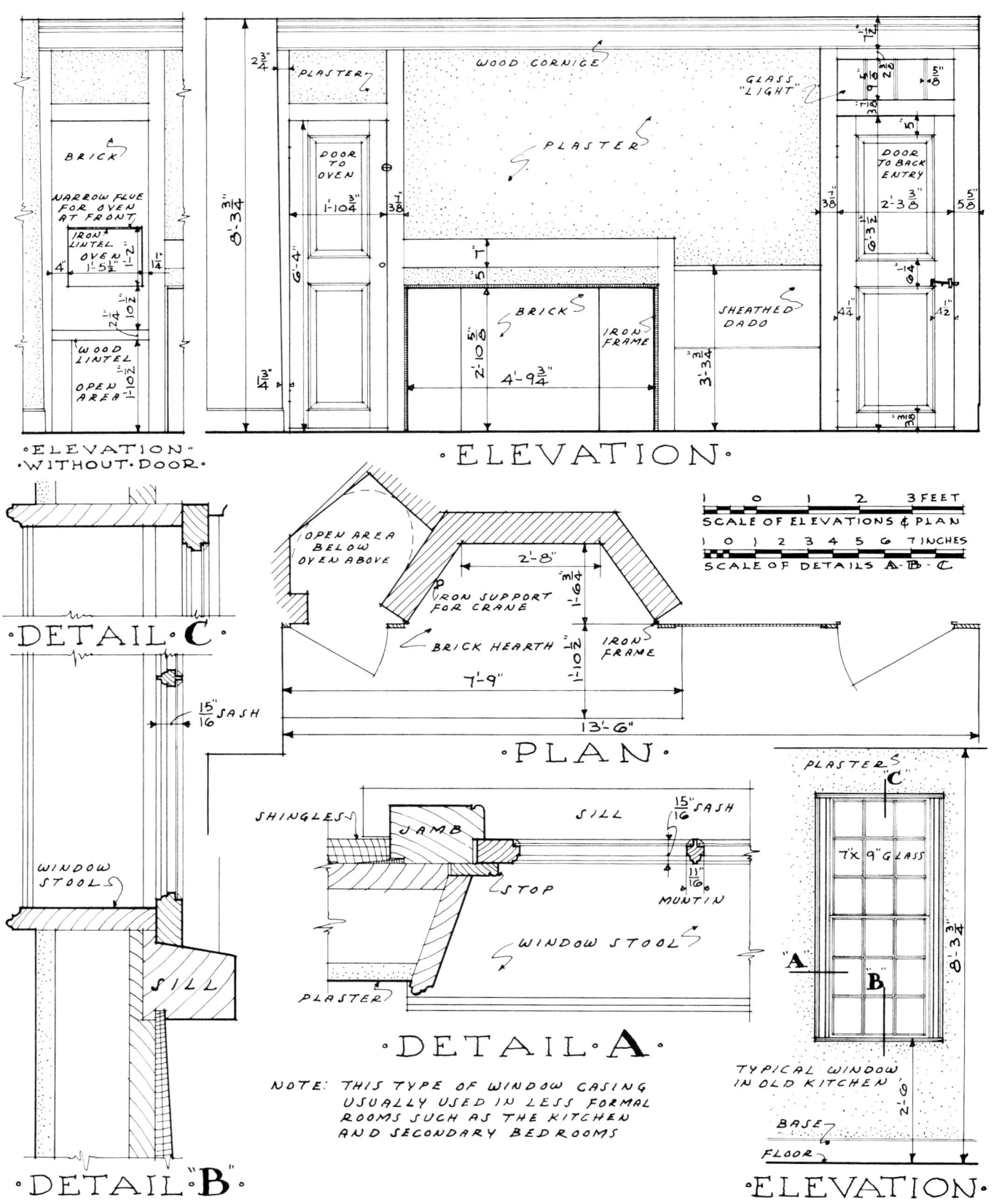

·ELEVATION· ·WITHOUT·DOOR·

BRICK

NARROW FLUE FOR OVEN AT FRONT

IRON LINTEL OVEN

WOOD LINTEL OPEN AREA

PLASTER

DOOR TO OVEN

WOOD CORNICE

GLASS "LIGHT"

PLASTER

BRICKS

IRON FRAME

DOOR TO BACK ENTRY

SHEATHED DADO

·ELEVATION·

·DETAIL·C·

OPEN AREA BELOW OVEN ABOVE

IRON SUPPORT FOR CRANE

BRICK HEARTH

IRON FRAME

2'-8"

7'-9"

13'-6"

·PLAN·

SCALE OF ELEVATIONS & PLAN

SCALE OF DETAILS A·B·C

$\frac{15}{16}$" SASH

WINDOW STOOLS

SILL

·DETAIL·"B"·

SHINGLES

JAMB

SILL

$\frac{15}{16}$" SASH

STOP

MUNTIN

WINDOW STOOLS

PLASTER

·DETAIL·A·

NOTE: THIS TYPE OF WINDOW CASING USUALLY USED IN LESS FORMAL ROOMS SUCH AS THE KITCHEN AND SECONDARY BEDROOMS

PLASTER

"C"

7"X9" GLASS

"A"

"B"

TYPICAL WINDOW IN OLD KITCHEN

BASE

FLOOR

·ELEVATION·

Old Kitchen (p. 114)

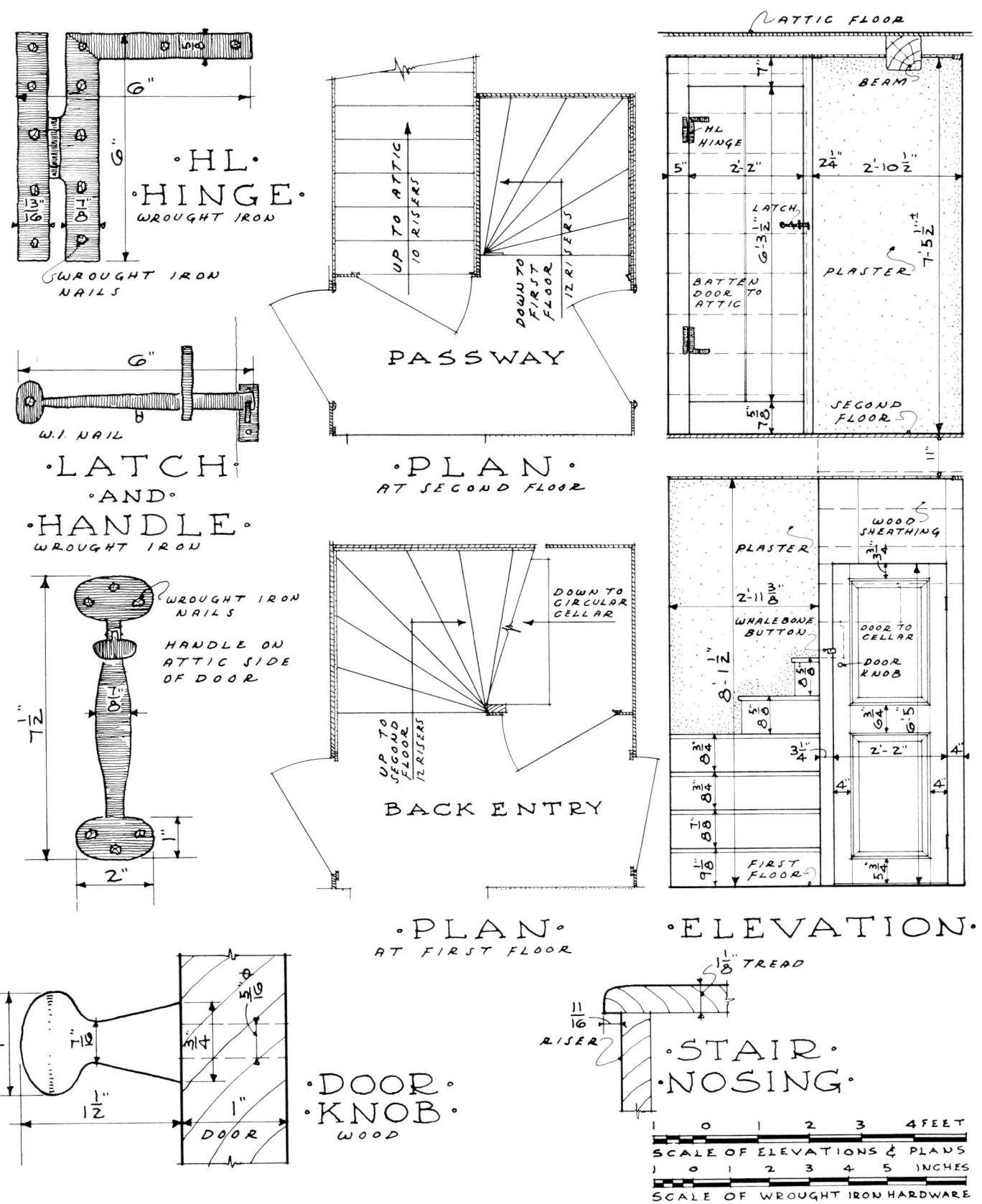

·HL· HINGE·
WROUGHT IRON

6"

6"

13/16" 7/8"

WROUGHT IRON NAILS

·LATCH· ·AND· ·HANDLE·
WROUGHT IRON

6"

W.I. NAIL

WROUGHT IRON NAILS

HANDLE ON ATTIC SIDE OF DOOR

7 1/2"

7/8"

1"

2"

·DOOR· KNOB·
WOOD

1"

8/5"

3/4"

1"

1 1/2"

DOOR

PASSWAY

UP TO ATTIC
10 RISERS

DOWN TO FIRST FLOOR
12 RISERS

·PLAN·
AT SECOND FLOOR

UP TO SECOND FLOOR
12 RISERS

DOWN TO CIRCULAR CELLAR

BACK ENTRY

·PLAN·
AT FIRST FLOOR

ATTIC FLOOR

BEAM

HL HINGE

5"   2'-2"   2 4/1"   2'-10 1/2"

6'-3 1/2"

LATCH

7'-5 1/2"

BATTEN DOOR TO ATTIC

PLASTER

5/8"   7/8"

SECOND FLOOR

11"

WOOD SHEATHING
3/4"

PLASTER

2'-11 3/8"

WHALEBONE BUTTON

8'-1/2"

5/8"   5/8"

DOOR TO CELLAR

DOOR KNOB

6 1/4"   6 5/8"

8 3/4"

8 3/4"

8 7/10"

9 6/10"

3 1/4"   4"

2'-2"   4"   4"

FIRST FLOOR

5 3/4"

·ELEVATION·

1 1/8" TREAD

11/16"

RISER

·STAIR· NOSING·

| 1 | 0 | 1 | 2 | 3 | 4 FEET |
SCALE OF ELEVATIONS & PLANS

| 1 | 0 | 1 | 2 | 3 | 4 | 5 | INCHES |
SCALE OF WROUGHT IRON HARDWARE

Rear Entry, Stair, and Second-floor Passway (p. 105)
The Isaiah Folger House   221

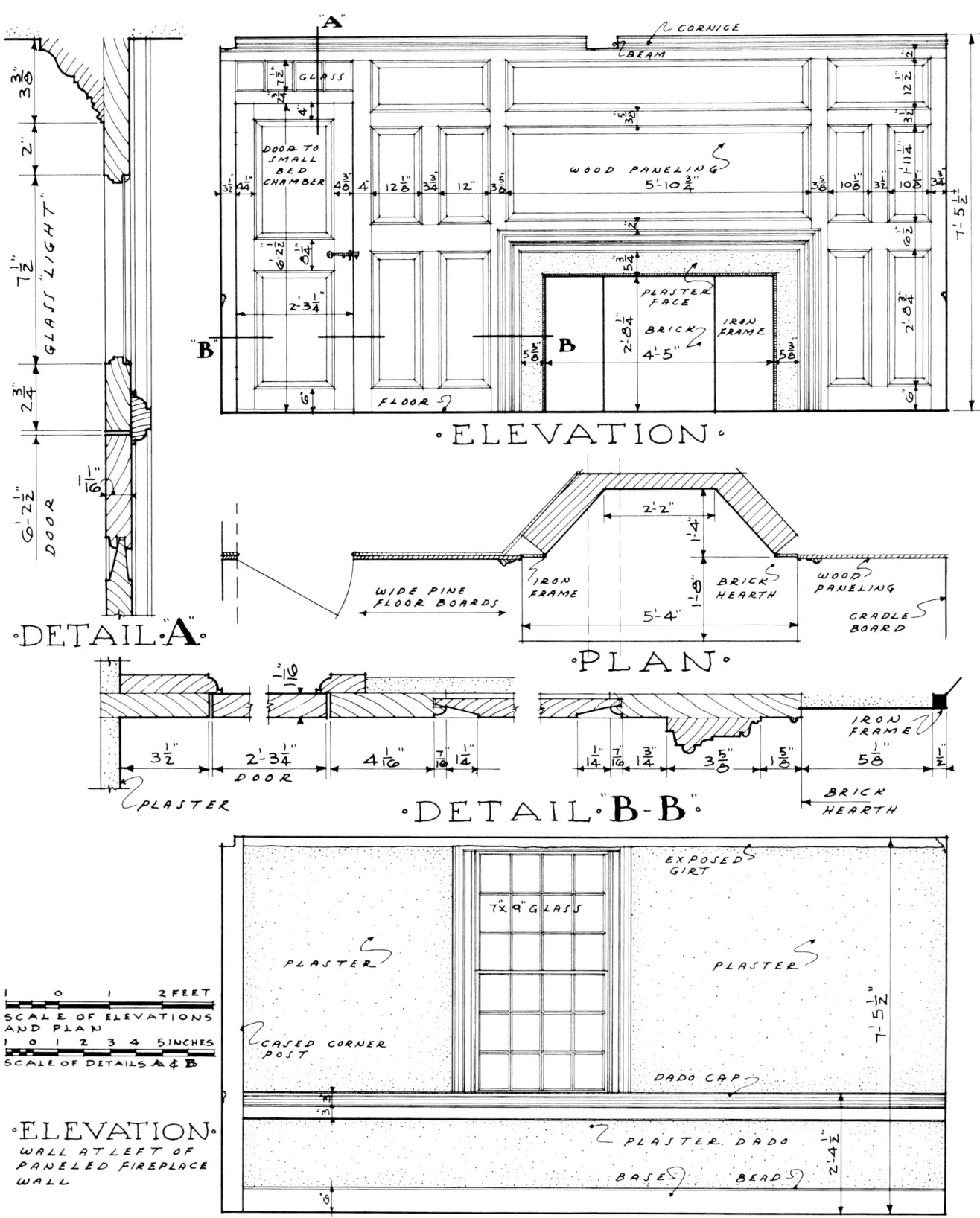

·ELEVATION·

·DETAIL·"A"·

·PLAN·

·DETAIL·"B-B"·

·ELEVATION·
WALL AT LEFT OF
PANELED FIREPLACE
WALL

SCALE OF ELEVATIONS
AND PLAN
SCALE OF DETAILS A & B

Second-floor Parlor Fireplace Wall (p. 108)

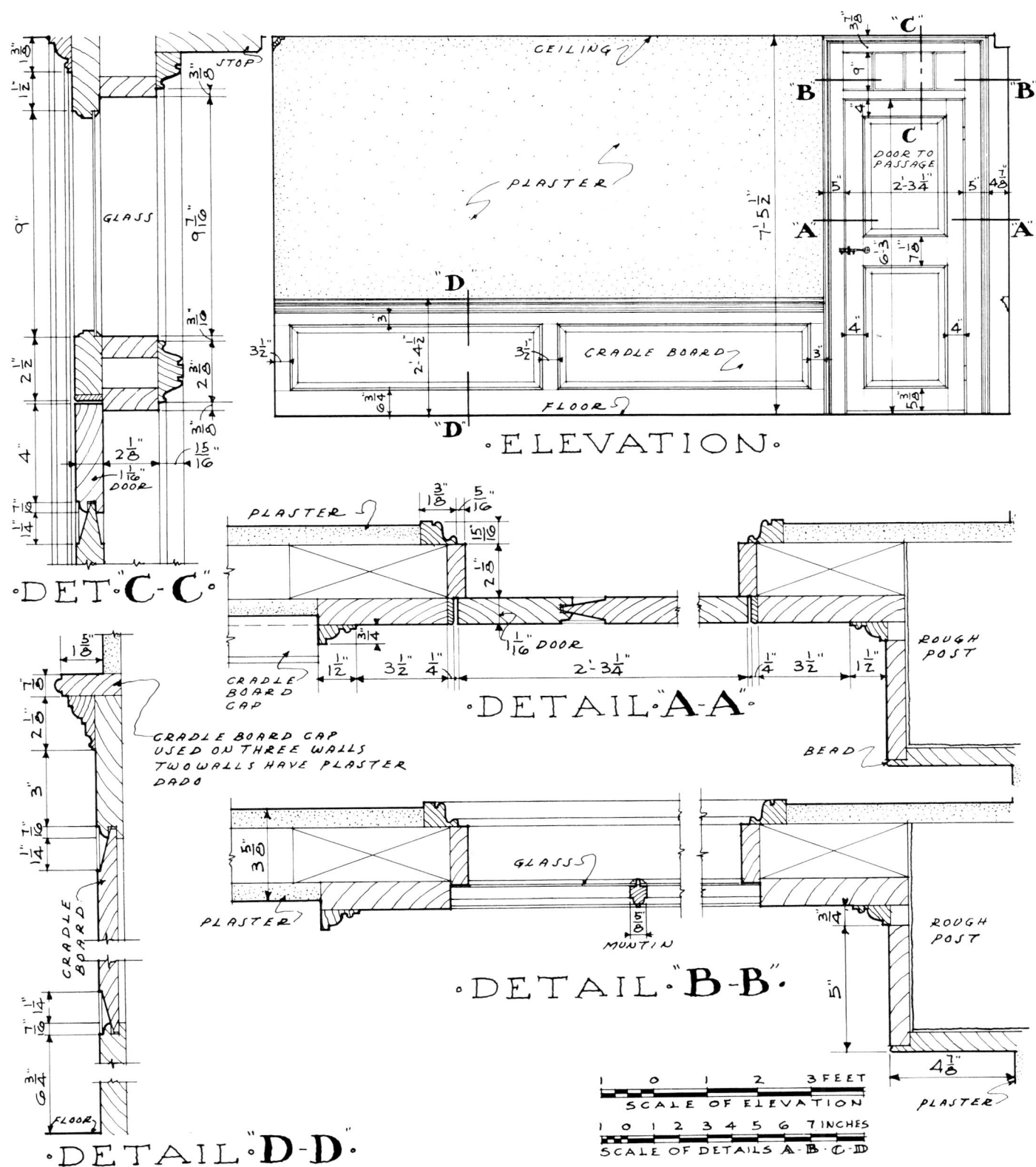

ELEVATION

DET "C-C"

DETAIL "A-A"

DETAIL "B-B"

DETAIL "D-D"

STOP

GLASS

DOOR

CEILING

PLASTER

DOOR TO PASSAGE 2'-3¼

CRADLE BOARD

FLOOR

PLASTER

CRADLE BOARD CAP

1 1/16" DOOR

CRADLE BOARD CAP USED ON THREE WALLS TWO WALLS HAVE PLASTER DADO

ROUGH POST

BEAD

GLASS

MUNTIN

PLASTER

ROUGH POST

PLASTER

CRADLE BOARD

FLOOR

SCALE OF ELEVATION
1   0   1   2   3 FEET

SCALE OF DETAILS A · B · C · D
1 0 1 2 3 4 5 6 7 INCHES

Second-floor Parlor Cradleboard Wall
The Isaiah Folger House   223

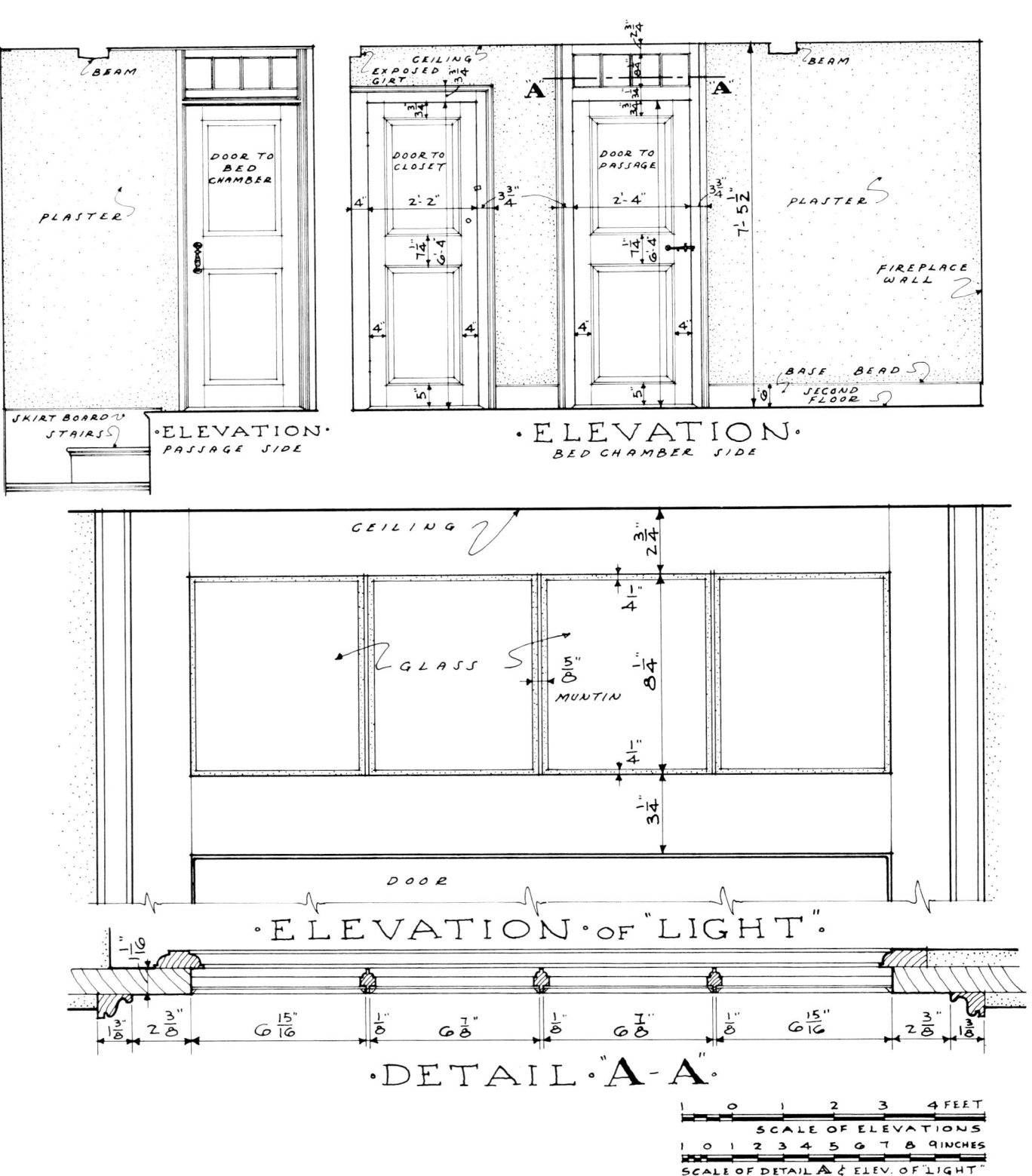

·ELEVATION·
PASSAGE SIDE

BEAM

PLASTER

DOOR TO BED CHAMBER

SKIRT BOARD STAIRS

·ELEVATION·
BED CHAMBER SIDE

CEILING EXPOSED GIRT

DOOR TO CLOSET

2'-2"

DOOR TO PASSAGE

2'-4"

PLASTER

FIREPLACE WALL

BASE BEAD
SECOND FLOOR

·ELEVATION·of·"LIGHT"·

CEILING

GLASS

MUNTIN

DOOR

·DETAIL·"A·A"·

0 1 2 3 4 FEET
SCALE OF ELEVATIONS

1 0 1 2 3 4 5 6 7 8 9 INCHES
SCALE OF DETAIL A & ELEV. OF "LIGHT"

Large Back Bedchamber (p. 107)

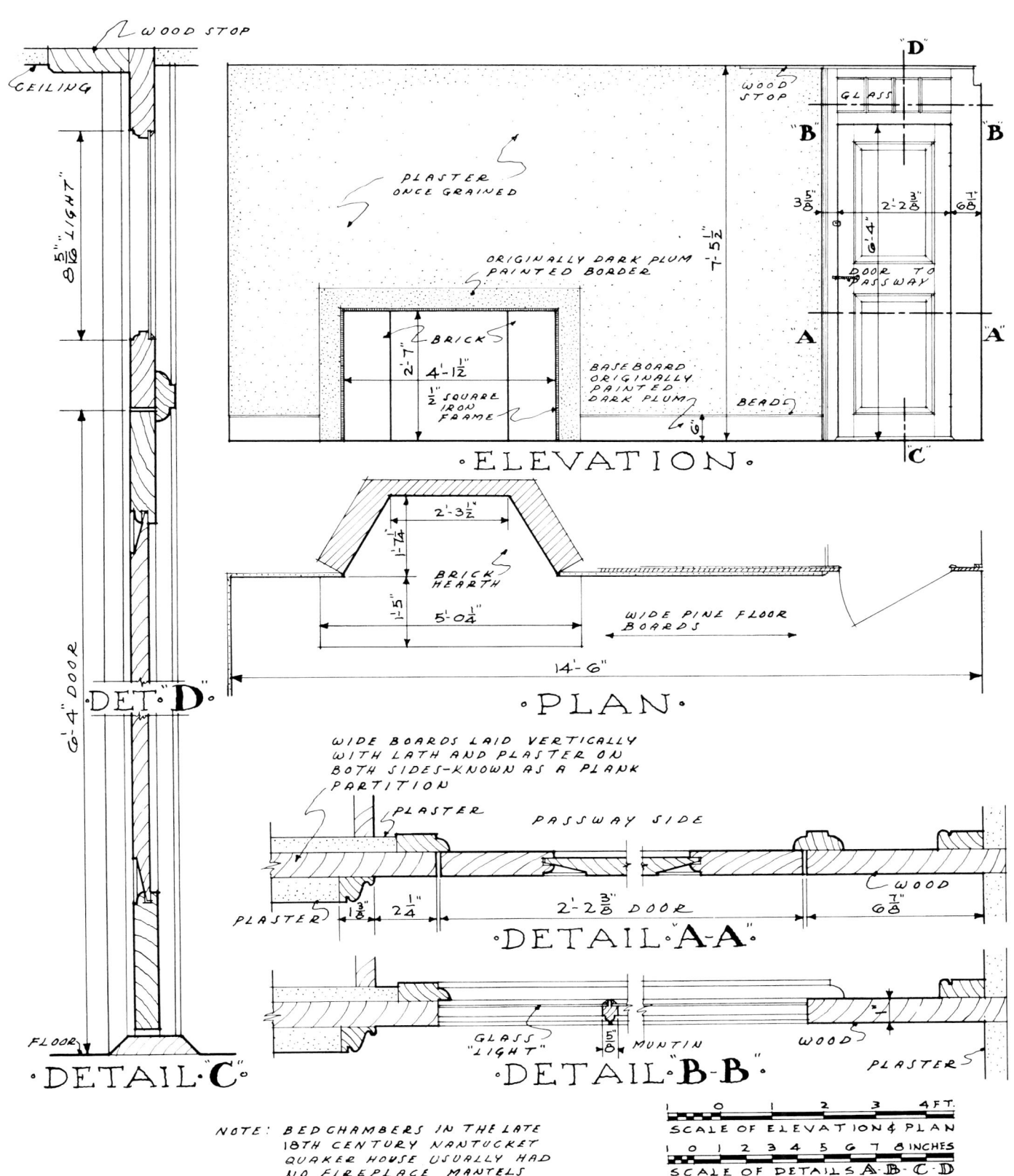

WOOD STOP

CEILING

8 5/16" LIGHT

DET "D"

6'-4" DOOR

FLOOR

·DETAIL·"C"·

PLASTER
ONCE GRAINED

ORIGINALLY DARK PLUM
PAINTED BORDER

7'-5 1/2"

2'-7"

BRICK

4'-1 1/2"

1/2" SQUARE
IRON
FRAME

BASEBOARD
ORIGINALLY
PAINTED
DARK PLUM

6"

BEADS

·ELEVATION·

D

WOOD
STOP

GLASS

B   B

3 5/8"

2'-2 3/8"   6 1/8"

6'-4"

DOOR TO
PASSWAY

A   A

C

2'-3 1/2"

1'-7 1/4"

BRICK
HEARTH

1'-5"

5'-0 1/4"

WIDE PINE FLOOR
BOARDS

14'-6"

·PLAN·

WIDE BOARDS LAID VERTICALLY
WITH LATH AND PLASTER ON
BOTH SIDES—KNOWN AS A PLANK
PARTITION

PLASTER   PASSWAY SIDE

PLASTER

1 3/8"   2 1/4"   2'-2 3/8" DOOR   WOOD
6 7/8"

·DETAIL·"A·A"·

GLASS
"LIGHT"

5/8"   MUNTIN   WOOD

PLASTER

·DETAIL·"B·B"·

NOTE: BED CHAMBERS IN THE LATE
18TH CENTURY NANTUCKET
QUAKER HOUSE USUALLY HAD
NO FIREPLACE MANTELS

1   0   1   2   3   4 FT.
SCALE OF ELEVATION & PLAN

1 0 1 2 3 4 5 6 7 8 INCHES
SCALE OF DETAILS A·B·C·D

Large Back Bedchamber, Fireplace Wall (p. 107)
The Isaiah Folger House   225

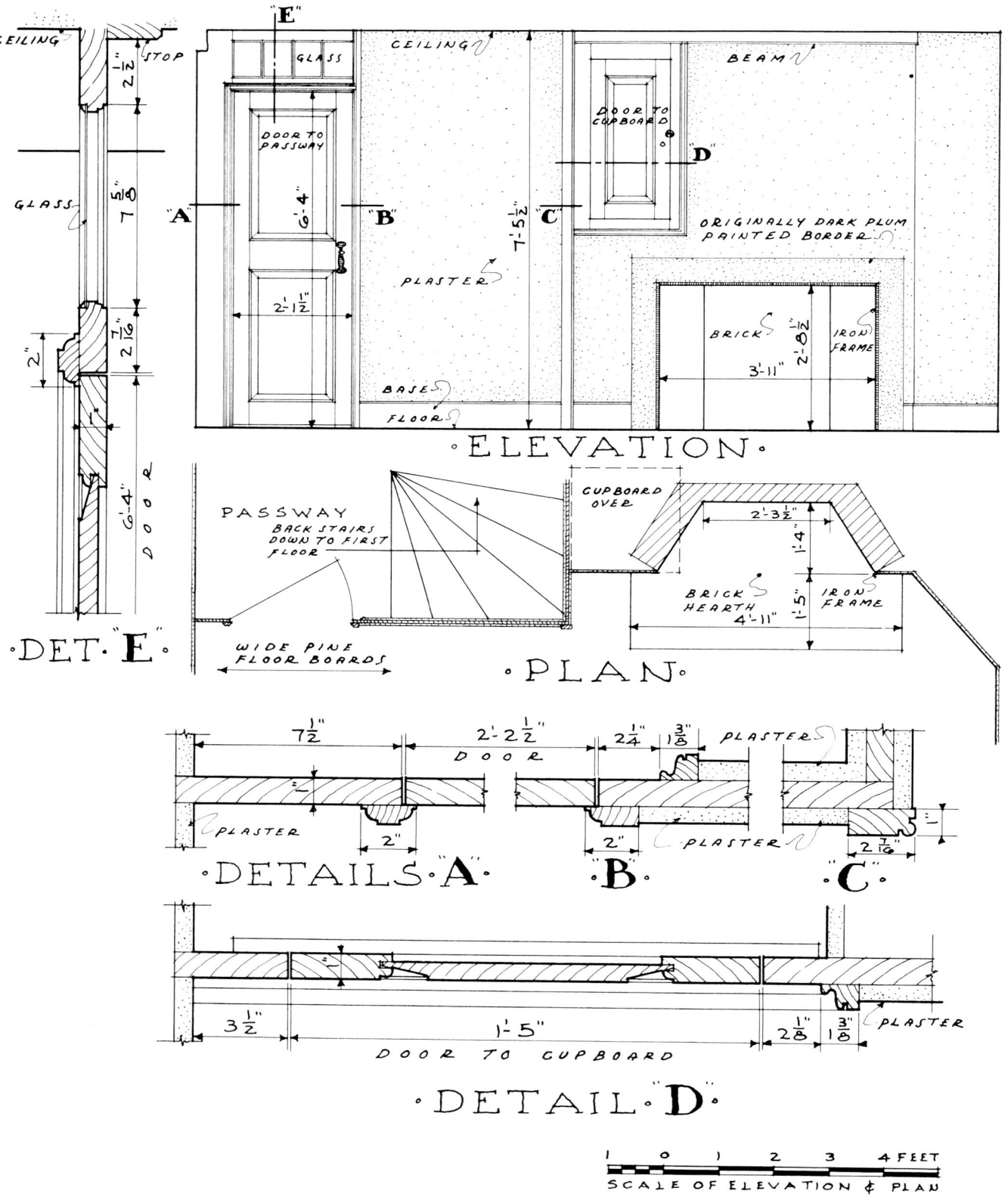

CEILING

"E"

GLASS

STOP

2½"

7⅝"

GLASS

"A"

CEILING

GLASS

DOOR TO PASSWAY

6'-4"

"B"

CEILING

BEAM

DOOR TO CUPBOARD

"D"

"C"

7'-5½"

ORIGINALLY DARK PLUM PAINTED BORDER

PLASTER

2'-1½"

BASE

FLOOR

BRICK

2'-8½"

IRON FRAME

3'-11"

2"

7⅟₁₆"

1"

6'-4" DOOR

· DET· "E" ·

· ELEVATION ·

PASSWAY

BACK STAIRS DOWN TO FIRST FLOOR

CUPBOARD OVER

2'-3½"

1'-4"

WIDE PINE FLOOR BOARDS

· PLAN ·

BRICK HEARTH

4'-11"

1'-5"

IRON FRAME

7½"

2'-2½"

DOOR

2¼"

3"

PLASTER

PLASTER

2"

2"

PLASTER

2⅟₁₆"

1"

DETAILS · A ·

· B ·

· C ·

3½"

1'-5"

2⅛"

3"

PLASTER

DOOR TO CUPBOARD

· DETAIL · D ·

1 0 1 2 3 4 FEET
SCALE OF ELEVATION & PLAN

1 0 1 2 3 4 5 6 7 8 9 INCHES
SCALE OF DETAILS · A · B · C · D · E

Small Back Bedchamber, Fireplace Wall

226   *The Isaiah Folger House*

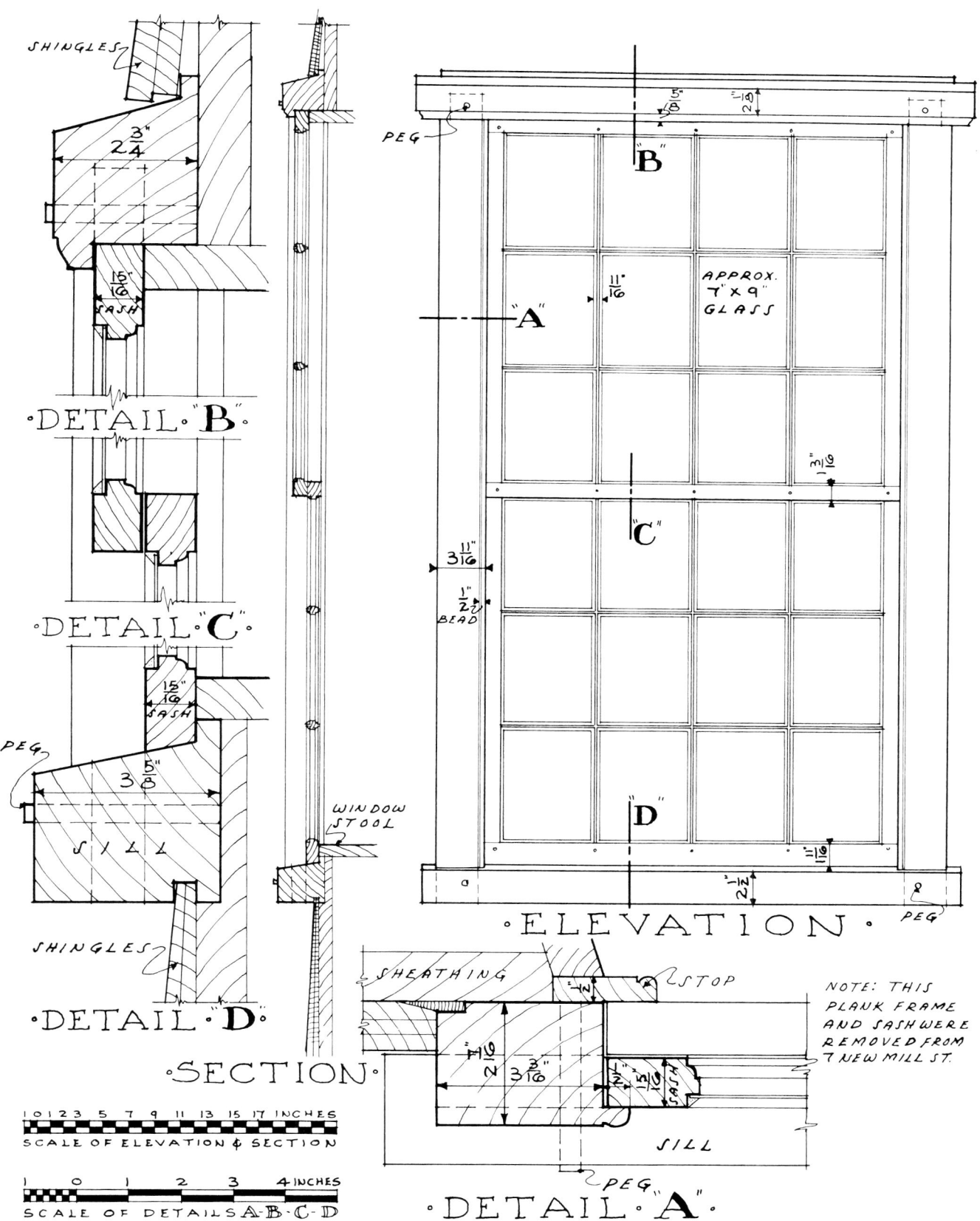

SHINGLES

2 3/4"

15/16"
SASH

·DETAIL·"B"·

·DETAIL·"C"·

15/16"
SASH

PEG

3 5/8"

SILL

SHINGLES

·DETAIL·"D"·

WINDOW
STOOL

·SECTION·

1 0 1 2 3   5   7   9   11   13   15   17 INCHES
SCALE OF ELEVATION & SECTION

1   0   1   2   3   4 INCHES
SCALE OF DETAILS A·B·C·D

PEG

5/8"

2 1/8"

"B"

"A"

11/16"

APPROX.
7"x9"
GLASS

1 3/16"

"C"

3 11/16"

1/2"
BEAD

"D"

1 1/16"

1"
2 2"

·ELEVATION·

PEG

SHEATHING

1 1/2"

STOP

2 1/16"

3 3/16"

5/16"
SASH

SILL

PEG

·DETAIL·A·

NOTE: THIS
PLANK FRAME
AND SASH WERE
REMOVED FROM
7 NEW MILL ST.

Typical Plank Window Frame and Sash   227

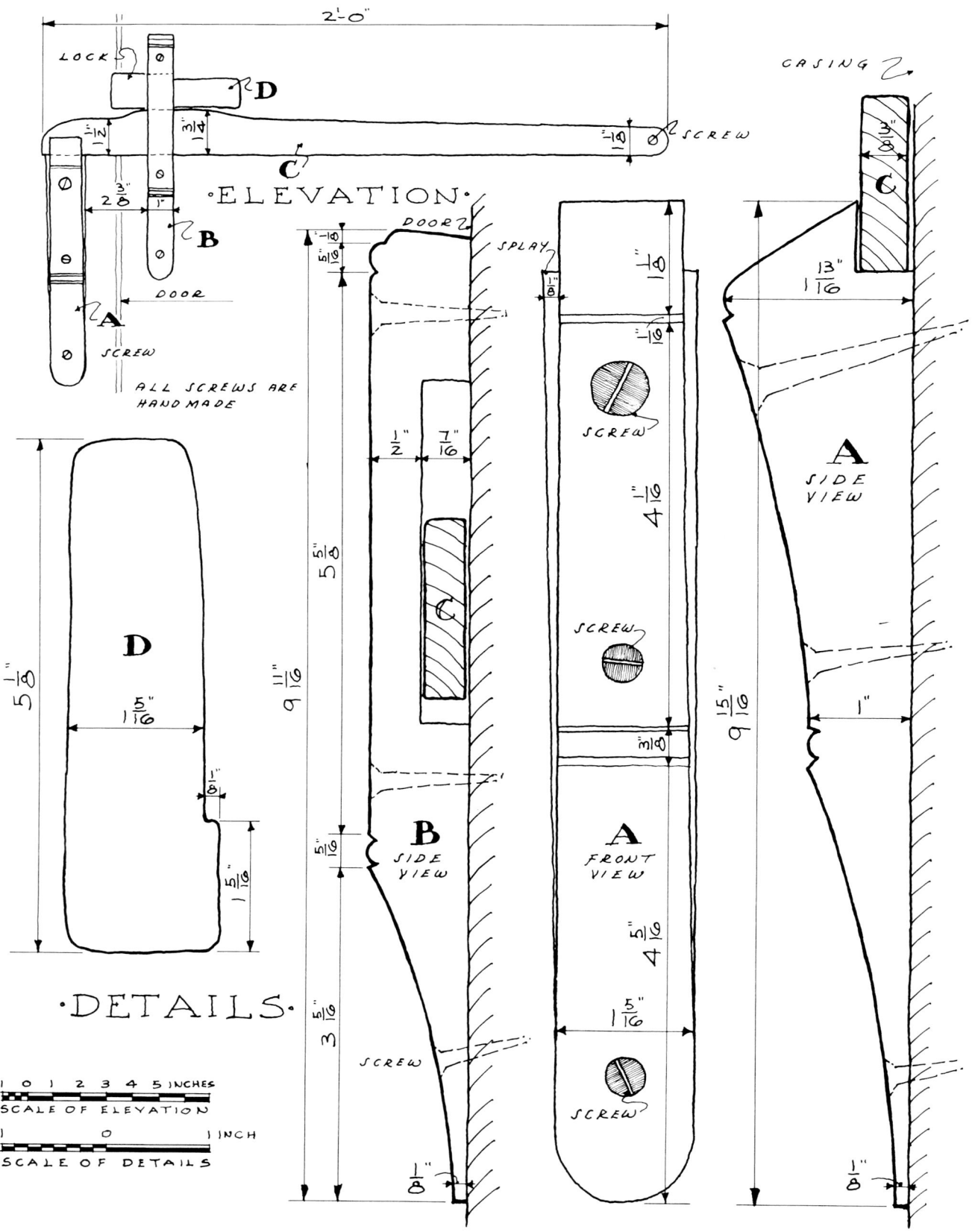

LOCK

D

·ELEVATION·

$1\frac{1}{2}"$

$\frac{3}{4}"$

2'-0"

$\frac{1}{16}"$ SCREW

CASING

$\frac{3}{8}"$

C

$2\frac{3}{8}"$ 1"

B

C'

DOOR

A

SCREW

ALL SCREWS ARE HAND MADE

DOOR

SPLAY

$\frac{1}{16}"$

$1\frac{13}{16}"$

C

$\frac{1}{16}"$

$1\frac{1}{8}"$

$\frac{1}{16}"$

SIDE VIEW

A

$\frac{1}{16}"$

$5\frac{1}{16}"$

$\frac{1}{2}"$ $\frac{7}{16}"$

SCREW

$4\frac{1}{16}"$

C

$5\frac{5}{8}"$

$9\frac{11}{16}"$

$5\frac{1}{8}"$

D

$1\frac{5}{16}"$

$\frac{1}{8}"$

$1\frac{5}{16}"$

C

SCREW

$\frac{3}{16}"$

$9\frac{15}{16}"$

1"

B

SIDE VIEW

$5\frac{5}{16}"$

A

FRONT VIEW

$4\frac{5}{16}"$

$1\frac{5}{16}"$

·DETAILS·

$3\frac{5}{16}"$

SCREW

SCREW

$\frac{1}{8}"$

$\frac{1}{8}"$

Front Door Interior Latch
228   *33 Milk Street*

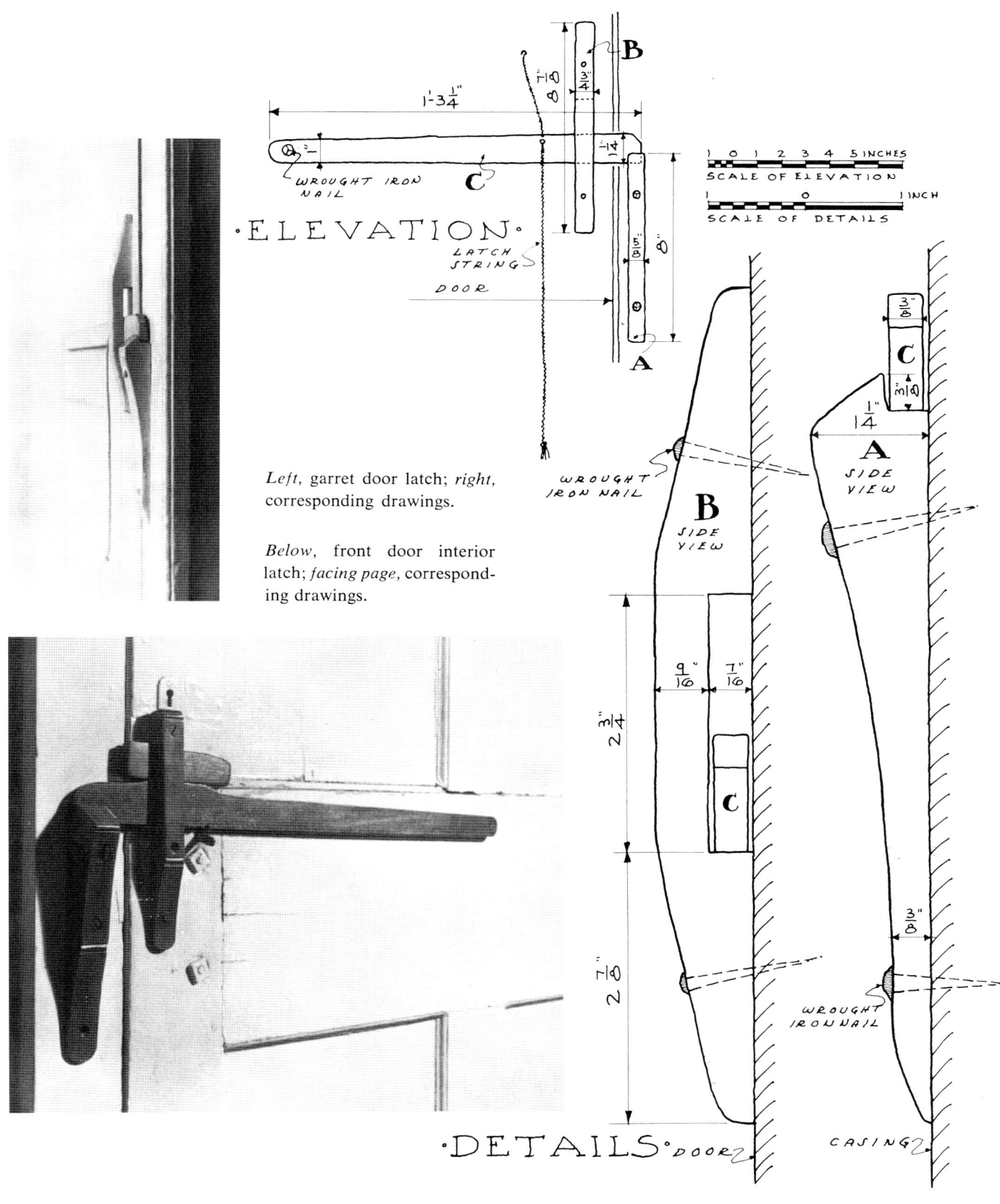

·ELEVATION·

1-3¼"

WROUGHT IRON NAIL

C

B

4½"○

⅛⅛"

1¼"

⅝"⅛

8"

A

1 0 1 2 3 4 5 INCHES
SCALE OF ELEVATION

1 0 1 INCH
SCALE OF DETAILS

LATCH STRING

DOOR

Left, garret door latch; *right*, corresponding drawings.

Below, front door interior latch; *facing page*, corresponding drawings.

WROUGHT IRON NAIL

B
SIDE VIEW

3"⁄₄²

9"⁄₁₆   7"⁄₁₆

C

⅛"⁄₈

2"⁄₈

C

⅜"

1¼"

A
SIDE VIEW

⅜"⁄₈

WROUGHT IRON NAIL

·DETAILS· DOOR

CASING

Garret Door Latch (p. 101)
The Maria Mitchell House   229

Parlor Ceiling Rosette (p. 213)
230   *9 Pleasant Street*

Glossary

ARCHITRAVE — Molded band surrounding a door or window opening.

BATTEN DOOR — Door made of vertical boards joined together with horizontal strips of wood called battens.

BEADING — Small, plain, semicircular-section molding often used at the joining of two boards.

BECKET — Woven rope handle on a sea chest.

BOLECTION — Important projecting molding used to frame a fireplace opening.

BORNING ROOM — Small room usually adjacent to the keeping room and behind the parlor. Being easy to keep warm, it was used for confinement during the birth of a child.

BUTTERY — Small pantry adjacent to the keeping room in which provisions were kept.

CAPITAL — Top member of a column or pilaster carrying the entablature.

CHAMFERING — Flat surface or bevel formed by planing off diagonally the angle made by the meeting of two right-angled surfaces.

CLASSICAL ARCHITECTURE — Architectural styles of Ancient Greece and Rome.

CLOSED STRINGER — Visible sloping member which supports the risers, treads and balusters of a stair.

COOKING OVEN — Oven built into the brickwork within or beside the recess of the fireplace.

CRADLEBOARD — Paneled dado on the interior wall perpendicular to the fireplace wall in the parlor of the typical Nantucket house.

CRANE — Swinging iron bracket in a fireplace for hanging cooking pots over an open fire.

CROSSETTED CORNER — Projection or ear at the corner of the molded casing around an opening.

DADO — The lower part of an interior wall set off by horizontal moldings.

DADO CAP — Molding which forms the upper part of a dado. Sometimes called a chair rail.

DENTILS — Equally spaced, rectangular blocks in a cornice molding, resembling teeth.

ENTABLATURE — Horizontal member in Classical architecture resting upon the columns and supporting the pediment. Each order of Classical architecture has its distinctive entablature made up of an architrave, frieze and cornice.

ENTRY — In Nantucket, a term used to designate a small entrance hall having a stair to the second floor.

FEDERAL — American period, coincidental with the early years of the Republic, 1780-1830.

FIRE BUCKET — Leather container for carrying water at a fire. In former times several hung in the front hall of each house, painted with the owner's name to insure their return after a fire.

FIRE HORN — Long horn used by fireman to announce a fire much as the siren is used today.

GEORGIAN — Decoratively, the period in England from 1714-1795, during the reigns of George I, George II and George III.

GIRT — One of a set of continuous heavy horizontal timbers in the exterior wall, supporting the second floor in a house frame.

GRAINING — Imitation of the grain of wood with paint. Often called featherwork because it was sometimes accomplished with a feather.

GREEK REVIVAL — Period of revived interest in Greek architecture which took place in America in the first half of the 19th century.

HALL — Early English term used to designate the room in which most of the daily living was done, now known as the kitchen.

HALL CHAMBER — Bedchamber on the second floor, directly over the hall.

HANGING STRIP — Narrow wooden strip on which pegs were mounted and let into the plaster walls in entries, passways and bedchambers in the Nantucket house.

JOISTS — Light, parallel timbers which support the boards of a floor.

KEEPING ROOM — Word used in 18th- and 19th-century New England to designate the room in which the family lived, cooked and ate its meals.

LEAN-TO — Addition built against a house, generally at the back.

"LIGHTS" — Glass transom over interior or exterior doors in the Nantucket house.

MIRROR BOARD — Narrow board or paneling on which a mirror was hung or supported between the two front windows in a Nantucket parlor.

MORTISE-AND-TENON JOINT — Method of joining two pieces of wood in which a projecting member on one fits into a sinking of like size in the other.

NANTUCKET COASTER — Small schooner from Nantucket used for shipping along the eastern seaboard.

NANTUCKET LIGHTSHIP BASKET — Type of basket made from fine cane by sailors stationed on lightships. The art has continued and there are basketmakers in present-day Nantucket. The baskets have become popular for handbags.

NANTUCKET SLEIGH RIDE — Enforced ride taken in a whaleboat towed by a harpooned whale.

NEWEL POST — Vertical member at the bottom or top of a stair into which the handrail is fastened.

OFF-CENTER HOUSE — Nantucket house with the front entrance placed off center in its façade, with two windows on one side of the door and one window on the other side.

ONE-SIDED LEAN-TO — Nantucket house of the lean-to type, having its entrance with one room beside it at the side of the façade.

PARLOR CHAMBER — Bedchamber on the second floor over the front parlor.

PARSON'S CUPBOARD — Small cupboard built into the area above a fireplace where the chimney slopes back. A wine decanter was often kept there for the refreshment of the visiting parson.

PASSWAY — In Nantucket, the narrow passage between two rooms, usually formed by the thickness of the chimney.

PILASTER — Rectangular column against and projecting slightly from the wall.

PLATE — Horizontal member on which the attic floor joists and roof rafters rest.

PORCH — Nantucket term given to the ell kitchen in a Siasconset cottage.

PROJECTED PLANK FRAME. Heavy window frame that projects beyond the face of an exterior wall of a house.

PURLIN — Beam carried by and perpendicular to the roof trusses or rafters.

REEDING — Small convex molding. Usually used collectively.

RISER — Vertical surface of a step.

SCRIMSHAW, SKRIMSHANDER — Objects carved by sailors from the bone or teeth of the sperm whale.

SHEATHING — Wide wooden boards applied vertically or horizontally to an interior or exterior wall as a finish. The joints are usually beaded or feathered on an interior wall.

SHED ROOF — Roof having only one slope.

SHIP'S KNEE — Also called breast hook, a wooden angle brace used in ship construction.

SILL — Horizontal member in the frame of a house, laid on the foundation wall to support the first-floor joists.

SILL (RAISED) — Sill that projects above the floor and beyond the wall into a room.

SKIRT BOARD — Molded wooden member fixed along the base of an interior wall and covering the joint between the wall and the floor. Also called a baseboard. Usually used in connection with a stair.

SPATTERED FLOOR — Floor that has been painted in a solid color and then spotted with other colors.

STRAP HINGES — Long wrought-iron hinges often used on batten doors.

SUMMER — Beam running perpendicularly to the girts and providing an intermediate support for the ends of the second-floor joists. It was generally the heaviest member of the framework of a house.

SUMMER KITCHEN — Kitchen used only in the warm summer months. Often found in the basement of a Nantucket house.

TRAMMEL — Pothook whose length could be adjusted by a ratchet arrangement when used in an open fireplace. In early New England the bar holding it was called a trammel bar.

VICTORIAN — Name given to the ornate, decorative style created during Queen Victoria's reign, 1837-1901.

VOLUTE — Spiral, scroll-shaped ornament used as an end to a handrail. Also the chief feature of the Ionic capital.

"WALK" — Platform built on the roof of a Nantucket house and surrounded with a railing. It is reached by a steep stair leading to a skylight or scuttle in the roof and is used to obtain a view of the harbor.

"WART" — In Nantucket, a small addition to a house. Used especially in connection with the Siasconset cottage.

"WATCH THE PASS" — In Nantucket, to observe from the windows the traffic passing by on the street and sidewalk.

Bibliography

ARCHITECTURE:

Crosby, Everett U., *95% Perfect: The Older Residences at Nantucket,* Nantucket, 1944

Halsey, R. T. H. and Cornelius, Charles O., *A Handbook of the American Wing, The Metropolitan Museum of Art,* New York, 1942

Hamlin, Talbot Faulkner, *Greek Revival Architecture in America,* New York, 1944

Hinchman, Lydia S., "The Maria Mitchell House and Memorial, Nantucket, Mass.," *Old-time New England. Bulletin of the Society for the Preservation of New England Antiquities, Vol.* XVI, No. 3 (January, 1926)

Kelly, J. Frederick, *The Early Domestic Architecture of Connecticut,* New Haven, 1924

Millar, Donald, *Measured Drawings of Some Colonial and Georgian Houses,* Vol. III, New York, 1930

Mixer, Knowlton, *Old Houses of New England,* New York, 1927

Poor, Alfred Easton, *Colonial Architecture of Cape Cod, Nantucket and Martha's Vineyard,* New York, 1932

Worth, Henry Barnard, *Nantucket Lands and Landowners (Nantucket Historical Association,* Vol. 2, Bulletin No. 5), Nantucket, 1928

FURNISHINGS:

Aronson, Joseph, *The Encyclopedia of Furniture,* New York, 1938

Bond, Harold Lewis, *An Encyclopedia of Antiques,* Boston, 1937

Nutting, Wallace, *Furniture Treasury,* 3 Vols., New York, 1948-49

Sack, Albert, *Fine Points of Furniture: Early American,* New York, 1950

Winchester, Alice, *How to Know American Antiques,* New York, 1951

HISTORY:

Blanchard, Dorothy C. A., *Nantucket Landfall,* New York, 1956

Bliss, William Root, *Quaint Nantucket,* Boston, 1896

Dell, Burnham N., "Quakerism on Nantucket," *Historic Nantucket,* Vol. 2, No. 3 (January, 1955)

Douglas-Lithgow, R. A., *Nantucket: A History,* New York, 1914

Hussey, R. B., *The Evolution of Siasconset,* Nantucket, 1912

Macy, William F., *The Story of Old Nantucket,* Nantucket, 1915

Stackpole, Edouard A., *Rambling Through the Streets and Lanes of Nantucket,* Nantucket, 1947

————, *The Sea-hunters,* New York, 1953

Starbuck, Alexander, *The History of Nantucket,* Boston, 1924

Turner, Harry B., *Nantucket "Argument Settlers,"* Nantucket, 1926

BIOGRAPHY:

Gardner, Will, *The Coffee Saga,* Boston, 1949

————, *Three Bricks and Three Brothers,* Boston, 1945

————, *The Clock That Talks and What It Tells,* Boston, 1954

————, *The Triumphant Captain John,* Boston, 1958

Kendall, Phebe Mitchell, *Maria Mitchell,* Boston, 1896

Shurrocks, Alice Albertson, *Two Steps Down,* Nantucket, 1953

MISCELLANEOUS:

Antiques Magazine, New York.

Austin, Jane G., *Nantucket Scraps,* Boston, 1882

de Crèvecoeur, Hector St. John, *Letters from an American Farmer,* London, 1951

Hayward, John, *A Gazetteer of Massachusetts,* Boston, 1846

Macy, William F., *The Nantucket Scrap Basket,* Boston, 1930

Stevens, William Oliver, *Nantucket: The Far-Away Island,* New York, 1936

Historic Nantucket, Nantucket Historical Association, Nantucket.

The Inquirer and Mirror, Nantucket.

Proceedings of the Nantucket Historical Association, Nantucket.

236

Index

Biography of Kenneth Duprey

MR. Duprey first came to Nantucket in the Spring of 1938, following his graduation from the Rhode Island School of Design. He instantly fell in love with the island and, in 1947, purchased his first house there. In 1961 he acquired another Nantucket house and spent the next four years restoring that property. In 1978 he moved permanently to Nantucket and spent the next two decades as a year round resident.

Perhaps Mr. Duprey's greatest legacy to his much beloved island is the Publication of this book, *Old Houses on Nantucket,* a photographic tour and informal study of Nantucket architecture. It has been described as an excellent guide for both the professional and the amateur interested in the preservation and restoration of old houses.